Connor Murphy discovered rugby in the USA early in his college career in the 1970s and continued to play for the University of Rhode Island for a few years after he graduated. In this affectionate and personal memoir he traces the development of rugby in the United States, from the early days when no-one was quite clear about the rules to intercollegiate championships and even major sporting events like the Olympics.

Covering not only the author's rugby career, but a concise explanation of the rules and US history of the game, the book includes a recollection of college life in the '70s (both sporting and social), aided by back copies of "The Good Five Cent Cigar" - the college newspaper, sporting programs, and yearbooks from the '70s.

Fascinating details such as the need for seasonal game clothing, the introduction of coaching staff, and what occurred at the post match parties add to the enjoyment of this book, a "must" for all US ruggers.

About the Author

Connor is a novice writer who tells true stories. His professional background consists of his previous work as a teacher and software developer. He graduated from the University of Rhode Island with a BA in Education. Connor enjoys sports of all kinds, and he and his wife Leslie (Jeannie in this story) currently reside in Rhode Island.

4

Connor Murphy

RUGBY TRIES
AND
KNOCK ONS

Tales of a college rugby player in New England and the game that gave birth to American football

AUSTIN MACAULEY PUBLISHERS™

LONDON ∗ CAMBRIDGE ∗ NEW YORK ∗ SHARJAH

A CIP catalogue record for this title is available from the British Library.

ISBN 9781786933348 (Paperback)
ISBN 9781786933355 (Hardback)
ISBN 9781786933362 (E-Book)
www.austinmacauley.com

First Published (2018)
Austin Macauley Publishers™ Ltd
25 Canada Square
Canary Wharf
London
E14 5LQ

Dedication

I would like to dedicate this sports book to all of our police and military personnel who protect our cities, towns, states, and country while providing us with our freedom and who are in harm's way every day. They are the warriors and heroes who fight the real "battles". This includes my dad, a Navy veteran of World War II who received the Purple Heart during combat.

I also share this story with my parents, Ed and Barbara, who supported me over the years with all the various sports I participated in since I was a child, including rugby – this very physical game that looks much more dangerous than it really is.

Extra, special thanks to my wife, children, and sister-in-law Lynne for putting up with many years of my rugby stories (although my wife lived some of it), and their support and comments concerning my previous book projects and this current book project that focused on the URI Rugby Club and my personal memoirs.

Acknowledgments

All photographs tagged with the "Cigar" or "Yearbook staff" literal are courtesy of the Special Collections and Archives, University of Rhode Island Library (URI). This includes *The Good 5 Cent Cigar* – the school's student newspaper, the *Grist* – the school's yearbook prior to 1972, or one of the University's "Renaissance" yearbooks I obtained while attending URI.

Other photographs were taken by individual fans and friends who attended some of these URI rugby matches. The inside team cover photo is courtesy of Steve Cote, a forward for URI and one of his friends who shot this early evening photo from 1976, the lone rugger in Chapter thirteen is courtesy of the Yearbook staff, and the "CONTENTS" page photo is courtesy of L. O'Neil. This photo is recent but shows a pair of my original rugby spikes and a Rhody practice ball that I kept after my career ended. These were both buried in an old box in my garage for many years. The rugby ball still had air in it, still playable.

The photo in Appendix H was also given to me by a URI fan and it shows me during some match downtime in my first full rugby season in 1976 and our fullback Doug Fay behind me, who was the last line of defense. The two University of Rhode Island Rams logos at the bottom of Chapter one and two are copyrights of one of the numerous athletic logos maintained by the University of Rhode Island.

Most of the information in this book is compiled from: *The Good 5 Cent Cigar*, "The Providence Journal" – Rhode Island's state newspaper, Wikipedia, various rugby websites (some cited), and memories from some of my teammates and myself who played in these rugby matches. This also includes the traditional rugby song's lyrics described in Chapter three, the various newspaper headlines in Chapter eight, and the New York Times article in Chapter six as well as the local Narragansett Times article in Chapter twelve.

The quoted "Cigar" article written by Bryan Ethier in Chapter thirteen is exact except the real names have been changed to match the rugger pseudo names in this true story.

I am grateful for playing this unique game created in England and spending time with so many great players, teammates, and friends during my college days. We developed a bond on the rugby field (pitch) that still exists today for some of these ex-ruggers even though the games have ended.

Special thanks to my teammate Bob Read who helped me fill in the blanks and supplied me with the technical jargon for many of the rugby rules and plays. He also provided me with some rugby photos from his college scrap book. Recently, I decided to write this book about our rugby team – I just needed more details that I couldn't remember by myself. It seems so long ago that I played rugby at the University of Rhode Island but during my actual writing and correspondence with Bob, it seemed like just the other day.

Bob Belluzzi also helped over the years with match details concerning our many opposing rugby teams, their players, and other assorted University of Rhode Island Rugby Football Club trivia and related information. This happened without my knowledge about the book that I hadn't planned to write during our regular rugby conversations over the years, when the Rhody Ruggers met at social gatherings. Bob remembers everything about URI Rugby!

10

Rugby Tries and Knock Ons
Tales of a college rugby player in New England and the game that gave birth to American football

Author: Connor Murphy

CONTENTS

PROLOGUE

The article above was posted in the sports section of *The Providence Journal,* the local Rhode Island newspaper, after the University of Rhode Island's 1979 New York Sevens Rugby Tournament win in late November but the score was incorrect. We won the final match with a score of 42 to 6. This sevens tournament was one of the first rugby sevens tournaments established in the United States in 1958.

This book details the growth and athletic maturity of the University of Rhode Island Rugby Football Club – a small college rugby team that played against other colleges and universities as well as men's rugby club teams in the seventies and early eighties. Many rugby college and university teams also competed against men's rugby teams during this time.

Some of these colleges and universities including URI coached themselves, maintained their fields where the matches were played, raised money to support the club, and created their own schedule of opponents to play against, except for special tournaments sponsored by larger rugby organizations in the area.

URI did supply our Rugby Club and other clubs with some minimal financial support that we used to pay for referees during each season. This book is not about winning or losing matches or championships. Instead it is a story about a "game" unheard of by many in the United States back in the seventies that my teammates and I played for the sheer fun, competition, and excitement of this game when many of us thought that our athletic careers were over. **Rugby has been called "the ruffian's game, played by gentlemen" and it is not for the timid.**

Some of the students that I played with on this university team were frustrated athletes who thought they had reached their athletic pinnacle during high school, or were cut from a major Division I sport such as football or baseball, or did not receive enough playing time in a Division I sport or club at URI. I think this contributed to the highly competitive attitude that many of the URI ruggers, including me possessed – we played this newly discovered game with a chip on our shoulders and hated to lose any match.

Some may have joined the URI Rugby Team because they enjoyed sports of any type especially a sport such as rugby that included a large social tradition of postgame parties, songs, and kegs of beer on the sidelines. The URI Rugby club consisted mostly of previous soccer, track, basketball, and of course football athletes who ventured into this English game. Nobody was ever cut from our rugby team although many did quit or were injured and never came back to the game.

At the high point of student participation in this club, the Rhody Ruggers as we called ourselves had almost three full teams. These teams were numbered as standard rugby levels: "A", "B", and "C" teams with the "A" team being the "varsity". There were no scholarships and little glory or press except for the local student newspaper – *The Good 5 Cent Cigar*. There was one year or two when one of our team members somehow hooked into the local state newspaper – *The Providence Journal,* and there were short news clippings of our major wins and losses in the sports section. Those that played this very physical game for the Rhody Rugby Team especially when we were at our best – winning many matches and being discussed throughout the New England Rugby circuit, **will never forget the team and its player's camaraderie… and of course the parties.**

This book was not written to brag about what we had accomplished during these years or how crazy some of the parties were. Remember these were the seventies and there were other college teams especially the Ivy League schools where rugby had been played for many years that were also good at this foreign game. The book was written for the love of a "game" played for fun, a thing of the past.

Today, there are so many organized sports for young children under the age of six, AAU and premier traveling teams, ultraserious and highly competitive recreation leagues, and parents searching for scholarships and professional contracts for their older children, during their athletic push for these children at the end of their sports pilgrimage. I believe many parents are also living some of their own lives through their children today due to their own sport failures or dreams that never materialized.

My daughter attended a summer camp one year at the University of Rhode Island when she was ten years old. It was a "fun" daytime only sports camp and she could choose a sport and a non-sport activity during this week. She chose soccer and art and had much fun at this camp.

At one of the parent meetings that they held to introduce the objectives of this camp, an informal speech was given by one of the camp administrators and I am paraphrasing this speech in my own words from what I remember. He asked all the parents in attendance to raise their hands if they competed in a sport during high school. The majority of parents raised their hands. Next, he asked how many parents competed in a sport during college. Fewer hands were raised but still a large number. The last question he asked was, "How many of you have played a sport at the professional level?" This time, very few hands were raised and he ended with another great point. "Let your kids experiment and play many different sports when they are young. Let them have fun and compete and do provide them with positive coaching activities such as camps and professional coaches but don't think of it as a path towards a sports career and a large pay check. Water seeks its own level and maybe, if your child works hard and has some special athletic talents, he or she might make it someday as a professional but many don't."

There was little press and few fans when I first started playing for this club team (Rugby was a club sport for the many men's teams as well that were not affiliated with a school.) but at the end of my career at URI, this had all changed. We had won many matches, competed at a national level in rugby sevens tournaments, won the praise of the local student newspaper due to our winning record, and we had many more students join this non-traditional club sport.

The friendships that I developed playing rugby still exist today, over thirty-five years later. The names of the URI ruggers I mention in this book are not their real names but our opponent names in this book are authentic. This was done because I spanned a few years of multiple rugby seasons with different players. We played both a spring and fall schedule and I would hate to leave anyone out of this book or forget a big moment with any of the players that I should remember. It's not because we behaved inappropriately or partied too much that I use pseudo names including my own in these short adventures. It's hard for me to mention each and every teammate that I played with back then due the number of different personnel configured teams that I was part of due to graduation, injuries, etc. I did add a list of many URI ruggers and their real names that may not be mentioned in this book but do appear in Appendix G.

There were also very few statistics back then. There was no Internet or social media and that might have been a good thing! Most of this book was created from memories and newspaper clippings that I saved from the student newspaper and *The Providence Journal*. We are all professionals now, some have retired from their work careers and most have families and children who did not witness us playing in this unique sport arena created in England in the eighteen-hundreds but still played worldwide today. There is also a possibility that rugby sevens, a version of rugby that we played and excelled at, may become an ongoing Olympic sport soon. It was recently part of the 2016 Olympic Summer Games and it is next designated for the 2020 Olympic Summer Games only.

This book is aimed at depicting the game of college rugby in a positive and fun light where everyone had a chance to compete and we taught and coached each other at practices and in matches. Nobody was left out or rode the "bench" no matter what skill level they possessed. Some readers may have some preconceived notions concerning the party reputation that the sport of rugby may have possessed back when I played but many colleges and universities had party reputations during those years unrelated to rugby. It was the sign of those times and the drinking age that was lowered to eighteen years of age that contributed to this party atmosphere.

Some of my teammates continued their rugby careers after graduating from URI, playing for their local city or town men's club where they settled after college. One of these athletes, Craig Keller, made the United States Eastern Sevens Select Rugby Team one year. This all-star team participated in the International Hong Kong Sevens Tournament when he played for the White Plains Rugby men's club during their regular fifteens season. Craig also played with the "URI Old Boys" sevens tournament team for many years. This was an all-star sevens team primarily consisting of URI rugby alumni who played for their local town's rugby club during the regular rugby season but entered special sevens tournaments in the off season.

Many of the backs that played for URI when I was part of this program also made some select/all-star rugby teams located in different parts of the country during their men's club rugby days after they graduated. This proved they were more than the typical beer drinking, knucklehead, college rugby player that seemed to be the stereotype in some people's minds back then and even today – they were very good athletes who became very good ruggers.

I left the game for various reasons after playing for almost six years at URI and one season with the local men's club – the Providence Rugby Football

Club (RFC). You didn't have to be a student to play on college teams back then but ninety percent of our team or more consisted of undergrad or graduate students. We even had one full-time professor, a high school exchange student from Spain, and a Westerly police officer who joined our club at different times. Rugby ended in my life when I grew tired of working low-paid jobs and needed a serious, full-time job with health care, a 401k, and other assorted benefits, not much different than today's goal of my children who have graduated college.

I then returned to school searching for a new profession rather than staying with the teaching career that brought me to URI that I didn't really enjoy at that time. I also discovered another sport towards the end of my rugby career that I also loved – martial arts. This new sport I participated in took up much of my free time – sixteen years of total training and teaching others. I used to point out to some of my rugby friends after I left the game that karate seemed almost less violent than the rugby matches I engaged in and had fewer injuries.

At the beginning of my karate training, I also played rugby for a few seasons. Tae Kwon Do was the style of karate that I studied and my chief instructor was Sensei David Arundel who owned and operated the school, a great teacher of the arts and a family man. He is also a high-ranking Kenpo instructor.

His wife Angela later taught at this same school - "Arundel's Academy of Martial Arts" when she achieved a high rank in the East Coast Tae Kwon Do Association that we were affiliated with, plus she earned more than a few Black Belt degrees years later. The very young students loved her and they gravitated towards her more than her husband. David sometimes scared the little ones because he was tall and had a loud, booming voice. Angela reminded them of their moms.

During those years that I competed in rugby at URI, I never realized just how good we were as a team or how good some of the teams were that we played, especially the sevens teams. I simply enjoyed going to practice every day after classes and being part of a sports team like I was when I played various other sports as a child growing up in Riverside, Rhode Island. Rugby has changed over the years and I don't watch many of the matches on television or in person but it was an important part of my life when I needed something in my life to help survive college and I continued competing in a sport for fun, camaraderie, and competition. **If you can't hit it, catch it, kick it, shoot it, or throw it – it can't be any FUN!**

I started playing rugby at the end of the 1975 spring season when many of the players had stopped attending practices due to injuries and exams and there was only one match left on the schedule. We played the majority of our matches as a club in fifteen-a-side rugby. The sevens tournaments we participated in were designated for certain team members only – who were mostly backs and we usually fielded an "A" and a "B" team at these special rugby events. Seven-a-side rugby consists of a faster paced game with much more running and features a small pack with three ruggers, usually those that have good speed and quickness. This type of rugby is played on the same size pitch that the standard fifteens game is played on. Sevens is a wide open match with passes flying across the pitch every which way and many one on one confrontations due to the few number of ruggers on the large field. It reminded me of basketball the way teams ran up and down the rugby pitch.

Without many of the veteran ruggers and most of us still practicing who had never played in a real match, we lost to Wesleyan University in that final fifteens match by a large margin. It was much different than the practices I was attending – rugby was very fast and very physical. I was unsure if I would be back the following fall season – but I did return.

We played much better in one of our early matches in 1976. In the "Cigar" photo below, I'm the farthest player in the background – waiting for the ball to come out after a "maul". Lenny Dawson is directly in front of me approaching the pack. The old jerseys we wore back then were white with light blue stripes throughout the entire shirt.

Cigar photo by Dave Corvese

The rugby club opened the season last Saturday in impressive fashion as they played the defending Yankee Conference Champions, Boston University, to a tie. This is some of the action from Saturday's game, played behind Keaney Gym.

CHAPTER 1

The beginning

"Just keep going. Everybody gets better if they keep at it."

Ted Williams – Hall of Fame American baseball player and Boston Red Sox legend.

Rugby is a style of football that developed in England at Rugby School and was one of the many versions of football or soccer-like games played at the various public schools in England in the early eighteen-hundreds. Rugby School is one of the oldest independent schools in Britain and was founded in 1567 by Lawrence Sheriff as a free grammar school for the boys who lived in the towns of Rugby and Brownsover. Rugby School today is a co-educational day and boarding school located in the town of Rugby, Warwickshire, England.

According to legend, the rugby version of running forward with the ball began in 1823 when a young man named William Webb Ellis, a student at Rugby School, picked up the ball and ran toward the goal. Prior to that, rugby consisted of kicking and catching the ball, but running forward with the ball was against the rules. The history of American football can be traced to these early versions of rugby football.

American football resulted from several major changes to the game of rugby. Walter Camp, a Yale and Hopkins school graduate is considered to be the "Father of American Football". He was a football player, coach, and sports writer. Among the important changes he made were the introduction of the line of scrimmage and downs and some distance rules. The year was 1880 when Walter set up these new rules for the game. The other major change was that the number of players was reduced from fifteen to eleven.

Edward "Eddie" Cochems was an early American football player and coach. Cochems played football for the University of Wisconsin from 1898 to 1901 and was the head football coach at a few different schools: North Dakota State, Clemson University, St. Louis University, and the University of Maine. During his beginning years at St. Louis, he was the first football coach to build an offense centered on the forward pass that many of us are familiar with today in the NFL. This forward pass became a legal play in 1906. Propelled by the forward pass, Cochems' 1906 football team compiled an undefeated record of 11 wins in that season and the team led the nation in scoring. Coach Cochems is considered by many historians to be the "father of the forward pass" in American football.

There are two main types of rugby today – Rugby Union and Rugby League. Rugby Union is the version of rugby we played. Rugby League is the other version which is similar to American football with "downs" or a specific number of times each team possesses the ball on offense. Both forms adhere to the same objective: getting the ball over the goal line or in-goal area to score points although some of the rules are quite different. In this book, I will be referring to Rugby Union whenever I mention the word rugby.

Points can be scored in rugby several ways: a "try" scored by grounding or "touching down" the ball in the in-goal area (between the goal line and the dead ball line) is worth 5 points (This scoring detail was changed from 4 to 5 points in 1992.), a subsequent conversion kick score is worth 2 points, and a successful penalty kick or a "drop goal" kick each scores 3 points.

May 1979 – Soldiers Field Stadium, Boston Massachusetts (Harvard Sevens Tournament)

"Another 'out of season' tournament that goes back at least to the mid-1960s is the Harvard Business School Sevens, held on a Sunday in early May each year. Little is known about the top 7s' teams prior to the mid-1970s: Washington, Old Blue, New York, Holy Cross, and Whitemarsh are names that come to mind as at least occasional 7s' winners.

In the modern era (late 1970s to present), the early sevens' powers in the East included the Duck Brothers, Bethlehem, **the University of Rhode Island (URI)** & URI Old Boys, Hartford, Long Island, and Roanoke."

Rugby7.com website

We had just beaten a few of the top men's rugby football clubs in the East that excelled in both sevens (seven players on the pitch) and fifteens (fifteen players on the pitch). This included Mystic River, Beacon Hill, the Washington Exiles, and two good college teams – Brown University and Coast Guard Academy. As I prepared for the championship final against another very good men's club – the Hartford Wanderers Rugby Club, I lay down on the sidelines and stretched my sore leg muscles. I didn't want to cramp up in this important final match.

My teammates had their own method of preparation – some jogging back and forth on the sidelines, some re-taping their fingers and wrists, others having a quiet conversation with other teammates concerning our next opponent. My mind drifted and I couldn't help but remember the previous three consecutive finals we had participated in. We had beaten some excellent teams each year to advance to the Harvard Business School Sevens finals, but we had lost each championship match. This rugby sevens tournament was the most popular sevens tournament in the East at the time and it consisted of rugby clubs, both men's and college teams primarily from the United States. There were no divisions or special categories back when we competed in this tournament – one division for all comers.

It could have gone our way in any of those tight matches, but it didn't. We were the University of Rhode Island Rugby Football Club, a college team consisting mostly of students and a few alumni including myself competing in a rugby tournament with teams of seven players on the pitch with no substitutions during each match. This tournament consisted of a few college teams and the best men's rugby clubs in the East but there were also a few men's rugby clubs from different parts of the United States and other countries.

I remembered playing the Denver Barbarians, a national powerhouse men's club in fifteens whom we lost to in the finals in 1978 and we would lose to them again in the 1979 National Sevens finals match in Hartford, Connecticut in June (Some rugby websites note that this was the first official National Rugby Sevens Tournament held in the U.S.). We played a team from England whom we beat quite handily in one of the preliminary matches in one of the previous tournaments. There was also a team from Belgium called the Brussels British that was knocked out of the tournament in 1978 – we beat them with a score of 28 to 4.

We had lost to the Hartford RFC in the finals, another men's club two years ago but now we had a chance for revenge. This was getting too familiar – losing in the finals each year. Maybe this was our time. The first year I played this version of rugby was in 1976 and we lost a tough finals match to Holy Cross College while holding on to a four-point advantage with only a few minutes left in the match.

It was almost dark on that late, cloudy afternoon and we had good defensive field position while hoping to score one last "try" and finish out the match and the tournament with Holy Cross. Holy Cross was pinned down close to their goal area but they still had possession of the ball.

One of their last offensives plays while on their own ten or fifteen meter line turned out to be the unexpected dagger that ended our great run. A pass meant for one of their running backs was dropped backwards or overthrown and a loose ball was available for either team. Most of our backs saw this opportunity and rushed for the ball. Somehow the ball took a crazy, sideway bounce and landed right into the hands of one of their outside backs. Most of our players including myself were caught flat footed or going forward past the ball so the Holy Cross player picked it up clean and then sprinted for the goal area with a good head start.

None of us had a chance to turn around quickly and catch the lucky opponent who proceeded to race for the try (four points for a try during my career) on a very long, uncontested run. I gave it my best but I couldn't catch him.

The two-point conversion kick after the try was also good. We were now down by two points with little or no time left on the clock. We had two or three more runs after they kicked off to us and then time ran out. Two college teams in the finals – I can't say that it happened before and it will probably never happen again at this highly competitive rugby tournament in Boston. (Note: Current rules for 15s – whoever scores, receives the ball on a kickoff. The rules for 7s – whoever scores, kicks off to their opponent.) I'm not sure that Holy Cross entered a team in the next three or four years we went to this tournament. I don't remember them reaching the semifinals after that first championship win and we never played them at the New York Sevens College Tournament either. This was another popular sevens tournament in the East held during the Thanksgiving college break and we dominated this tournament as well with many wins and championships. This tournament was different though, separated into two distinct divisions – college teams and men's club teams. Many colleges would pay the nominal entrance fee and enter this special tournament to test their rugby skills and prowess against other colleges only.

The referee called the captain of each team out onto the pitch and a coin was flipped. We won the toss and elected to receive. This would be a very tough match for us especially now that Barry Richards played for the Hartford Rugby Football Club. Barry, a URI alumnus moved to Hartford the previous year to work for his father-in-law and to be close to his wife's family. He had played for four years on the Rhode Island Division I football team as a defensive back and the story that I was told was that Barry had a walk-on tryout with the New York Jets NFL team. He didn't make the team but the Jets loss was our win. Barry visited our team one afternoon in late March at one of our practice sessions and immediately started playing rugby for us. After graduating from URI, he became a teacher and coached football at South Kingstown High School close to the university campus so he only played in the spring seasons for our rugby club. He was strong and very fast and played the other wing opposite me in standard fifteen-a-side rugby for URI.

Barry played rugby for many years and was chosen for various select side rugby teams during his career and even played with some "Old Boy" clubs (ruggers over 35 or 40 years of age). He stopped playing rugby when he was fifty years old and I'm guessing – he was still in great physical condition then.

In this finals match, I would have to mark him and try to make sure he did not have a good game. Of course he would have to mark me and try to stop me from scoring. The kick was deep and Reed Reynolds, who was considered part of the scrum in this sevens version of rugby, but played wing and outside center as a back in fifteen-a-side rugby, handled the long kick...

The "Cigar" photo below was taken during one of our earlier matches of the spring season in 1976 – my first full year of rugby. As the newspaper clipping describes - we ended on a high note with six out of seven match wins and we lost to Holy Cross in the finals of the Harvard Sevens Tournament in Boston. That was not a high note for most of us that day even though we did beat some great men's clubs.

Cigar photo by Dave Corvese

This is some of the URI rugby action in an earlier game this season. The ruggers completed a successful season with six wins in their last seven games, and finished runner-ups in the Harvard seven's tournament last weekend. See story on page 13.

CHAPTER 2

My journey

"That was a great time. I was in my 20s, had lots of energy. I have great memories of it."

Ringo Starr – Famous English drummer, singer and songwriter, and one of the surviving two Beatles, the best band ever.

May 1975 – University of Rhode Island Rugby field, Kingston Rhode Island

I caught the funny, oblong-shaped ball and then ran wide to the left side of the rugby field. Two players lunged at me but I sped past them and ran into the "in-goal area" or end zone for American football readers. I touched the rugby ball on the ground in the middle of the goal area. A try or score has to touch the ground while the player has control of the ball when in the rugby goal area or the try does not count. I scored my first try – but this was only a practice with nine players versus nine. On this day, both teams ran up and down the pitch many times and there were many missed tackles as the ball was dropped, bobbled, and fumbled in between the various tackles, trips, and falls. Right away, I enjoyed playing this new game but on that day, there was not much contact. I was fine with this because I had never played football and did not really know how to hit or tackle the opposing team's players, but I could run. It was the end of the season and many of the better ruggers were missing.

My speed had increased over the last few years – I guess I had physically matured late after high school. I competed in track and field in high school, running middle-distance races and also triple jumping and was a little better than average. I ran for the URI track team during my sophomore year for one indoor season. The team wasn't very good and I struggled as well – running the 600 yard individual event and a 440 yard leg on the mile relay team in the "Bubble". The "Bubble" was an old cinder track built inside a large rubberized bubble type of structure that was popular in the seventies. I was glad that a few of our meets were cancelled due to snow; I was tired of getting my butt kicked in individual races. (I think I would have been better suited running the 100 and 200 yard events that occur in outdoor track.)

Those days have changed for the URI Track team. Head Coach John

Copeland and his consistent, hardworking men's teams have won five out of the last six Atlantic Ten Division I Indoor Track Championships. They have a number of other championship banners in the Mackal Indoor Field House where they compete and Coach Copeland was recently voted Eastern Regional Coach of the Year. The women's track team is also very talented and had two All-American weight throwers on the team a few years ago – Crystal Bourque in 2011 and Jasmine Jennings in 2009. I was looking for something else to keep me busy during college downtime so I tried playing this strange game invented in England that I knew little about when I first saw a few ruggers practicing. Some of these students had long hair and cut-off jean shorts and they were running up and down on one of the fields behind the gymnasium. Their attire seemed quite odd for rugby players but this was the seventies.

Some of these students did not look very athletic so I decided to show up at one of their practices at the very end of the season to see how I could fare against them. It reminded me of a game many young boys had played in the local fields or neighborhood back yards where I grew up in Riverside, a section of East Providence – it was called "muckle". It was a form of American football and depending upon the number of players on each team that given day, differed considerably as far as real football rules. Some games featured no passing, some games had no blocking, sometimes we played two-hand touch rather than tackle, etc.

I attended a few more rugby practices and relished this new game that I had heard of but never played. Speed seemed to be a key factor in rugby and both teams had ample time controlling the offense so I had many opportunities to break away from the other defenders I played against in those early practices and scored a try or two. I was faster than I thought on a rugby field, maybe being chased by larger opposing players contributed to my speed. Back then, I did not like to get hit but in rugby, contact was plentiful and a large part of the game. The fine art of tackling and responding after getting tackled would be skills I would have to acquire soon if I continued playing this game.

Most of our team consisted of ex-football athletes and they knew how to tackle and hit hard but without helmets or pads and players working both sides of the ball, rugby was a much different game than football. Long sleeve jerseys with a white collar was the main uniform we wore but in the early years of building a competitive team, most of our rugby team didn't wear official rugby shorts or rugby spikes. We looked out of place sometimes when playing the men's club teams and the Ivy League schools where the teams only wore real rugby gear and rugby spikes. We were colorful to say the least – wearing basketball or gym shorts, all with different colors and football spikes or cleats.

I looked worse than anybody on our team back then as far as appearance in rugby attire. Whatever jersey I wore, I cut the sleeves off so it fit like a regular short sleeve t-shirt; the tight sleeves of most rugby jerseys constricted some movement in my arms and hands. One year, I also had my sister Mary remove the collar from my jersey and sew back what was left but that didn't work out so well. One or two tackles while wearing that shirt, and the shirt ripped down the back side. The "no collar" look physically weakened the jersey. I was ahead of the times then because most rugby game jerseys now have short sleeves and no collars or a "mini" collar type of crew neck.

Socks in those days also varied, but most of the Rhody Ruggers wore the special rugby, soccer, or basketball socks that hung just below the knees. Not me. I wore plain, long, white athletic socks but I loosened and crumbled them so they fit just above my ankles. This floppy sock "look" was popular with Pete Maravich during the same years when he played basketball in the NBA. I don't remember if I copied him or created this rugby fashion style on my own.

I also wore green colored shorts for my Irish heritage. I thought that was a great color to wear in my early playing days but it was an ugly match that didn't go with our Rhody light blue striped, colored jerseys that we wore at that time. I also failed to realize with my speed and green shorts – I became easily recognizable on the pitch and a target for any opponent we played. A target is not something you want to be on a rugby field – fifteen opposing players ready to take a shot at you at any time. There are no separate offensive or defensive positions in rugby and at that time, there were no substitutions. It is similar to soccer – all players playing on both sides of the ball at all times, offense and defense.

The major rule of rugby is very simple – all passes must be sideways or backwards and cannot be thrown forward to a player but you can kick the ball forward. Other rules such as when you can handle the ball when it is on the ground or what designates a penalty, etc. are more complicated. After playing for many years, I'm still not sure I know all of them and many of the rules have changed since my playing days. They have substitutions now, a penalty box called the "sin bin" and yellow cards. Two yellow cards and you are expelled from the match.

A kickoff starts each match. Both halves of the match begin with a drop kick from the center-point of the halfway line of the pitch. After a player is tackled and the ball is on the ground or the ball is stuck in the middle of a standing tackle, a few things can happen. A "scrum" is called by the referee (Scrums occur when both teams' forwards or pack get together over the ball and the ball is placed into the middle of the scrum to start a new play.) when he feels the ball is not going to come out or release whether it's on the ground or held up in a standing tackle. If a scrum is called, then a rugby back called the "scrum-half" rolls the ball into the tunnel formed between the two opposing packs or scrum (similar to offensive lineman in football) and whichever team pushes the hardest would then control the ball and another offensive play would begin but only when the ball comes out.

Tackling that results in a player going to the ground usually follows up with a "ruck" with the opposing players trying to push (ruck) over the ball that the tackled player must release when he is on the ground. It cannot be touched with hands until it is clear of the ruck that is formed. "Air over the ball" describes when a ruck is clear. Tackling that results with a player holding the ball which does not go to the ground and the player remains standing and not moving forward, usually results in a "maul". A maul involves players from both sides as they encircle the player who has possession of the ball. The maul ends when the ball either hits the ground or the player in possession of the ball emerges from the maul. The thinking in rugby terms is that if your team created the ruck or maul with the ball, you have to "get it out". Rules for rucks and mauls have changed somewhat since I played many years ago.

If a penalty occurs during any action on the pitch that warrants a penalty, the team that did not commit the infringement are given possession of the ball and a player may either kick it towards "touch" – out of bounds over the sidelines that then determines a "throw-in" from the sidelines by the other team, attempt a place kick at goal (If the kick is successful, then 3 points are scored.), or tap the ball with his or her foot through an invisible "mark" and then run the ball.

A key position in the scrum is a called a "hooker". He is positioned in the middle of the scrum, held up by two players called "props" on each side. The hooker "hooks" the ball back towards his team while his forwards try to move the other forwards backwards.

It can be a verbal signal from the scrum-half or a hand movement (tap) from the hooker himself when the ball is put into the tunnel of the scrum and the hooker strikes at it with his leg to hopefully send it back through the scrum for the scrum-half. It's a special timing scenario between the scrum-half, hooker, and pack to supply their team with possession of the ball. This has all changed now. There are three verbal commands called by the referee – crouch, bind, and set. On the last command, the scrum-half then rolls the ball into the tunnel and both packs fight to push over the ball and win possession.

Once the ball pops out of the scrum – and it must be a "clean" out – the scrum-half starts the offensive play by either running the ball or passing the ball backwards to another back called the "fly-half" that is similar to a quarterback in football. He can also kick the ball forward or "skip" the fly-half and pass to one of the other trailing backs, if it warrants that type of play. *Forward passes and dropping the ball forward that are called "knock ons" are both illegal in rugby.* A scrum is designated for these slight infractions and for any other minor infractions of the rugby laws or rules. The team that did not commit the infraction is allowed to put the ball into the scrum.

At this point when the ball does come out of the scrum, anything can happen and the ball can then be passed to any of the backs or forwards who usually form a horizontal line as they jog or run towards the opposing team's goal. Players can also kick the ball forward to move up and down the pitch, but only teammates who are behind the kicker can then race after the live ball and pick it up. The other ruggers on the same team can only move forward and handle the ball after the kicker passes them to allow them to be "onside" and now they are considered in play and can pick up the ball.

We played a home match against a top university rugby football club from Newcastle, England – whose hooker hooked and controlled the ball with his head. I never played in the scrum so I'm not sure how a player does that but they controlled the ball most of the match. (This is not allowed anymore in rugby, too dangerous.) On that game day, I spent most of my time chasing and tackling the opposing backs. We lost the match but we did beat them up pretty good with our non-rugby method of tackling. Real rugby tackles consist of grabbing and holding players and tackling standing up so as to keep yourself and the ball in play. Instead, we would leave our feet sometimes like American football and try to knock down the opposing player with great force. This meant that the tackler was out of the play as well as the opponent we hit for some time until both recovered from the ground tackle. When we did this, the ball might fly loose and you never knew who would possess it, as compared to rugby tackles that consist of controlling the ball with standup hits and grabs and stripping the ball from the opposing player if possible.

The defending backs of the opposing team who are usually matched against each corresponding offensive back can then field the kicked or fumbled ball (Knock ons continue a play only if the opposing team picks the ball up.) and start their offense in motion when they possess the ball. The positions of the backs in rugby from start to finish as they line up behind the forwards or pack are: scrum half, fly-half, inside and outside centers, wing (two wings, one on each side), and full-back.

Another key player in rugby matches who handles the majority of kicks in a match is called a "full-back". He patrols the middle of the pitch usually positioned behind his own backfield. This position is also very important for both offense and defense and is similar to a safety in football or a sweeper in soccer. This full-back must be adept at kicking the ball and sometimes handles many of the extra points after a try and penalty kicks that are similar to a field goal in football that count for three points.

We played against a great Boston Rugby Football Club men's team in a few New England open rugby tournaments and their full-back had a kicking tryout with the New England Patriots. (The New England Patriots were called the Boston Patriots prior to 1972 for all of the younger readers.) He was very good and played with a purpose but we didn't like him very much because he kicked the ball for good field position most of the time and we never had much of a chance to tackle him or rough him up because he released the ball so quickly. He also wore a turtleneck under his jersey, sometimes even in the warmer weather – not sure what that was all about. But unlike football, any player in the match can kick extra points or penalty kicks, not just the designated kickers.

Providence to host rugby tournament

PROVIDENCE — For the third consecutive year, the Providence Rugby Club will host the New England Rugby Football Union Tournament at Hope High School. The tournament begins tomorrow at 10 a.m. with the championship game scheduled for 2 p.m. Sunday.

In addition to the host team, Brown University, the University of Rhode Island and the Boston Rugby Club, the defending champion, also will compete.

Other teams entered are:

Beacon Hill Rugby Club; Hartford Wanderers R.F.C.; Portland Rugby Club; Concord, N.H., Rugby Club; Berlin, Conn., Strollers; Charles River Rugby Club; Harvard Business School; Mystic River Rugby Club; Dartmouth College; the University of Massachusetts; Amherst College, and Boston University.

The Providence Journal article above mentions the men's clubs as well as some of the colleges that competed each year in the New England RFC Tournament that URI participated in during my career. We never made it past the semifinals and seemed to lose to Boston each year – they were tough!

Two of the full-backs with whom I played the majority of my matches at URI were very different athletes. Doug Fay weighed about 190 pounds and had a solid build. He had a great foot and kept us in many matches with his defensive kicking prowess and difficult conversion kicks and goal kicks for points. These goal kick attempts can occur after a penalty and are similar to field goals in American football. He played during my early years when we were just learning the game and most of us were very rough around the edges with our rugby skills. He was another great high school athlete on our team who played football and wrestled on one of the first Coventry, Rhode Island championship wrestling teams in 1972.

This wrestling program had one of the longest high school championship spans in the country at one point in time. They won seventeen state titles in a row from 1982 through 1998 a few years after Doug graduated. One of his teammates on this high school team also attended URI and was recruited for wrestling for this very good Division I college program. He was an All-American in the mid-seventies in his senior year. His name is Scott Pucino and his brother Frank was also a tremendous wrestler at Coventry High School and the University of Rhode Island. I have two other friends whom I met at URI who also wrestled on this nationally ranked team – John Staulo and Jimmy Urquhart. John played football, lacrosse, and wrestled for URI and Jimmy just missed making the USA Olympic wrestling team after his senior year. He also helped coach the team after he graduated while working on his master's degree. John is in the Massachusetts Coaches Hall of Fame and Jimmy is in the URI Hall of Fame. They were both great collegiate wrestlers and fun guys to hang out with. The coach for this very good team who brought them into the national spotlight was Alan Nero.

Alan was a 1969 graduate of Springfield College and also a former college wrestler. His teams won three New England championships and four conference championships and he was named New England Coach of the Year three times.

Paul Thayer was the other full-back who was thin and had a wiry build who covered the rugby field as a full-back but did much less kicking and more running than Doug. Paul was a good defender and tackler but his speed and quickness gave us an added punch in the backfield because his style of play meant that we had a third wing or another outside center on the pitch. He was an extra offensive weapon in matches and an integral part of our later sevens teams.

Drop kicks are another weapon that can be used anytime during a rugby match when a player is running on the pitch and on opening kick offs. I never saw too many of these attempted for a score in all of the matches I played and I never attempted one myself. Instead, I went for the corner of the goal line nearly every time I received the ball. Due to my lack of size – five foot ten and 168 pounds, I disliked cutting back towards the middle of the pitch or running inside plays close to the scrum or larger backs. I played "wing", a position similar to a wide receiver in football. You didn't have to be big.

This was the last position across the pitch in the rugby backs lineup. The wing's primary function is to finish off moves and score tries. Wingers are usually the fastest players on the team and are either elusive runners or big and strong power runners who are able to break tackles. Most of the time, they run wide towards the sidelines and try to score in the corners of the goal area. If they are larger, more physical wingers, then they can also cut back against the grain of the defense to try to score if a lane is open or run straight up the rugby field and try to run over other backs.

Wings were also sometimes the last player in the backfield to touch the ball on a given play. This would happen if the play went all the way "out" when our backs didn't cut back to the inside past the opposing backs, when they didn't kick the ball for field advantage or a defensive play, or when they didn't pass the ball to one of the scrum players who were usually moving straight up the pitch after their work was done pushing the ball out. At times, my style of rugby was one-dimensional – I tried to score and I tried to stop the opposing wings or centers from scoring.

Our team had plenty of speed including the forwards so most of the time our fly-half, Rob Calissi who was a terrific high school quarterback and baseball player out of Roosevelt High School in Yonkers, New York would try to distribute the ball to our outside centers and wings. He was also quick and had great inside running moves so he could fake a pass to the outside and then blow by his defender for large gains and keep the ball movement in our favor. Sometimes, he would also throw a long pass backwards to the outside center or wing (skip pass). I never saw anybody else perform this football quarterback pass in fifteens for the five or six years I played. It was common in rugby sevens though – due to the small number of players on the pitch – and it was less dangerous to lose the ball in this version of rugby mayhem.

When we drove close to the other team's goal, any player could score a try – back or forward but I loved to score, especially when I received a pass with only ten or fifteen meters between myself, my opposite defender, and the goal line. I would try to make the most of these one-on-one situations the more I played this crazy game and the more experience I gained with each match. I scored five tries against a dismal Cortland State club one season and at one point in the match I tried not to score when an opponent stood me up with a high tackle two meters from the goal area and I still controlled the ball.

I waited for one of my teammates to catch up to the play so I could pass him the ball and allow another Rhody Rugger to score a try. It was taking too long and my opponent started wrestling the ball from me but I won the ball back and fell over the goal line and touched the ball down for my last try.

In other sports – if you are beating an opposing team by many points – you can substitute and play your second or third string players – but not in rugby when I played. Substitutions were established after my career had ended.

Many ruggers both in the pack and the backfield did much of the hard work to push the ball up the pitch but many times the outside centers or wings including Barry, Reed, Jay Tagliardi, and I would receive the credit with a short, final dash and try at the end of a drive. This is how I obtained one of my nicknames when I played rugby at URI – "garbage man", but I also scored more than a few tries on very long runs. I have to say it was a great feeling when you broke a long one and you touched the ball down in the middle of the goal area and both teams are just watching you jog back to your teammates before the two-point conversion is attempted and the ensuing kickoff. There were no end zone dances or hoopla when we scored in rugby.

I did get too excited once during my second season at URI during a home match with UMass who had beaten us in a small college tournament the previous season. I spiked the ball on the ground after a breakaway score with a great pass from the outside center that day. The next time I had the ball, I saw all fifteen players in a rage come after me. I was tackled out of bounds and a major pileup of my opponents trying to punch and kick me ensued. Somehow, I wasn't hurt and I crawled away from the mob. Most of the team's punches hit their own players. That was the last time I ever spiked a rugby ball.

Rugby is similar to hockey in that respect – ruggers police their own game. If you make a "dirty" play against a player on the opposite team, someone from that team can and will retaliate. In rugby, you play offense and defense and are always on the rugby field so it's easy to be returned the "favor" for any unaccepted action on the pitch. As I explained before, there were no substitutions when I played rugby.

Most of the backs and some ruggers in the pack, especially the "number eight" players who can release from the pack and run with the backs also scored tries. But the centers and wings seemed to score the most for our team – that was our style of play. We were a track team playing rugby, as some of the men's clubs labeled us. The men's clubs we played against seemed to play the opposite way, more of an inside scrum game with ball control by the large forwards that these teams possessed and much more kicking. Most of the time, we were outsized by these large men's teams in the scrum so we had to defend well. We then used our speed as an advantage to make the most of our limited chances to score a try if that was the scenario when we possessed the ball – and we did, especially in those rugby sevens matches.

URI featured many ex-football players who then became rugby players when their football careers ended. The NFL features a few players with the opposite sport scenario – playing rugby in their early years and then switching to football after rugby ended. Today, there are a few ex-rugby players who are playing football in the NFL.

Nate Ebner is one of these NFL veterans. He played rugby while a student at Ohio State and played football as a walk-on for his school as a defensive back and special teams' gunner during his junior and senior years only.

He received a tryout with the New England Patriots in 2012 after he graduated and currently plays safety and special teams for them. He has been with the Patriots for the past four years and now owns a Super Bowl ring after the 2015 Championship year and had many key tackles and plays during that season. The Patriots took Ebner with the 197th overall pick despite the fact that he had played just three snaps on defense in college. He played rugby in high school, not football and was the youngest rugby player selected for the U.S. National Sevens Team at the age of 17.

The New York Jets previously experimented with Hayden Smith, a former rugby player signed by the Jets in 2012. Smith played tight end for New York but spent most of that 2012-2013 season on the practice squad. He did appear in five games and recorded a reception for 16 yards but was released prior to the next season. Hayden began playing rugby in 2008 with the Denver Barbarians RFC and then joined the professional English side – Saracens Football Club. He was also a regular with the United States Eagles Select Side.

In the photo below, I'm breaking a long one for a try on our home field against an unknown opponent. (It might have been the select side from France.) You can see in the background that the URI baseball players were watching us and enjoying the action. Our field at one point was next to their field. Both teams had a game that day. (Photo by G. Desisto)

CHAPTER 3

Postgame parties and "Chicago"

"Rugby is great. The players don't wear helmets or padding; they just beat the living daylights out of each other and then go for a beer. I love that."

Joe Thiesmann – American NFL commentator and Washington Redskins Football quarterback legend.

During my rugby days at URI and with the local Providence RFC men's team, there existed the traditional post "match" party with the visiting team. The home team would supply the beer and maybe some wine for the few females who attended the party at a local clubhouse, bar, fraternity, etc. This was very common then but may not exist today for most of the college teams and **definitely does not occur with the current University of Rhode Island Rugby Club.** (They may have their own unofficial party or gathering for the older ruggers only.)

This may be due to the current drinking age in most states – twenty-one years of age. The drinking age was twenty-one in my junior year of high school but that changed sometime after, primarily due to the Vietnam War. This drinking age law change occurred when the war became much more intense and many more young soldiers were killed or could be killed in combat but yet, they could not order a beer or wine at a restaurant or pub when they were off duty. That's why this law changed, for obvious reasons.

These parties added another dimension to the sport of rugby but also caused some new issues that could affect the team. Sometimes, these parties would get somewhat out of hand and players who survived the match that day might get injured during the party festivities. These simple parties included various games where drinking was a factor and festive songs and light conversation with the opposing team took place after each team tried to knock the stuffing out of the other team, only a few hours previously. This is unheard of in any other sport contest.

One of the more popular drinking games at these parties consisted of the typical "boat race" where a set number of players/drinkers would be selected from both teams and placed at a table or bar area in close proximity to each other while standing or sitting. At the start of the "race" called by an official referee (any player from either team), each drinker would chug a full beer from a mug or a glass. After the team member completed the final sip of his drink, the next drinker from that same team would then chug his beer and so on until the last drinker completed the final pint and slammed his mug or glass down on the game table to complete the boat race and hopefully ahead of the other team's last player to win this event.

There was another drinking game called the "Muffin Man" and this consisted of one very athletic drinker on each team, who while still in full uniform, would place a full cup of beer (Mugs and glasses were too dangerous to use even for ruggers.) on the top of his head and at the official "start" of this race would proceed to take his shorts, jersey, socks, and spikes off while balancing the beer on top of his head. I think you needed to possess a flat head to even attempt to be involved in this game. I never competed in this game.

If the beer spilled, the participant would have to chug a fresh beer and then another full cup of beer would be placed on the player's head by one of his own teammates. This went on until the first player who successfully removed all his clothes and then chugged the cup of beer that hadn't spilled on top of his head was deemed the winner. There was also a song that went with this game that was similar to the traditional nursery rhyme or children's song of English origin but I'm guessing you might know that the lyrics were quite different and "R" rated.

Another drinking game that many of the ruggers and some of our party guests seemed to enjoy was called "Sink the Titanic". This game consisted of placing a large empty beer glass in the middle of a full pitcher of beer and one player at a time from each team would then take turns filling the glass with beer from a different pitcher while trying to keep the glass floating inside the original pitcher. Both ruggers and fans were allowed to play this game. This would continue until the glass was "sunk" – that is when it could not float any more in the pitcher.

The player or fan that caused the sinking of the "Titanic" would then remove the full glass of beer and drink it down. (This was a little unhygienic when the person removed the glass while placing his hands in the pitcher of beer to remove the glass but it didn't bother most of the ruggers who participated.) No winners were recognized in this game – just plenty of hooting and hollering and shouting out the title of this game "Sink the Titanic!" and other similar phrases by the participating crowd. There was no pitcher limit or time limit on this particular drinking game.

No prizes were awarded for any of these drinking game victories other than pride in a party game "win". Some teams we played lost the Saturday match on the pitch but unofficially won the party especially in the early years when we were novices at the party competitions – but we always concentrated more on the rugby field victories.

Sometimes, there were also some variations of rugger streaking events during these parties. Streaking was a craze that popped up on college campuses and high schools during the seventies but I won't detail any of that.

Over the years, the URI Rugby Football Club played against many different colleges and men's teams and we never played the same schedule twice. During these matches and post party festivities, we learned many traditional rugby songs and sang them at all our home game parties whether we won or lost. The most popular and favorite song that we overdid in my later years at URI was the *Chicago* song. This song was funny and had a nice beat to it but was also a little vulgar as some of these rugby songs were – and sometimes some of the Rhody Ruggers took it to a whole other level.

We tried to save this song for the end of the night when many of the opposing team members or fans had left for the evening because once we started, we never ended the song with the number of verses we would come up with. I know many of the players actually prepared for new and creative verses prior to matches even if they didn't make any sense – rugby homework. This song turned out to be a "party killer" and even the visiting teams who were used to any rugby song would become disgusted with the total repetition of this simple song and walk out of the party.

The *Chicago* song had one basic verse that was repeated with a change to the object or person that was being inserted into the verse. Below are just a few verses that existed in this obnoxious song during the singing activities. It could get somewhat inappropriate as you can see from the sample lyrics below and I'm sure you understand where this song is going.

I won't say I was one of the ring leaders of some of these silly songs and I could add new verses to keep a song going too long at the parties just to annoy the opposing team but I did receive the "Lawrence Welk" award one year when rugby certificates were awarded to some individuals for various skills on and off the rugby field. Mike Tagliardi and his brother Jay seemed to be the creators of these certificates; Jay's signature is on the one certificate that I received in my rugby scrap book.

I Used to Work in Chicago – sung to the tune of *For He's a Jolly Good Fellow*

I USED TO WORK IN CHICAGO IN A DEPARTMENT STORE,
I USED TO WORK IN CHICAGO, I DID BUT I DON'T ANYMORE

A young lady came into the store looking for a camel
A camel FROM THE STORE?
A camel she wanted, hu... She got
I DON'T WORK THERE ANYMORE!

I USED TO WORK IN CHICAGO IN A DEPARTMENT STORE,
I USED TO WORK IN CHICAGO, I DID BUT I DON'T ANYMORE

A young lady came into the store looking for some fireworks
some fireworks FROM THE STORE?
Fireworks she wanted, ba... She got
I DON'T WORK THERE ANYMORE!

I USED TO WORK IN CHICAGO IN A DEPARTMENT STORE,
I USED TO WORK IN CHICAGO, I DID BUT I DON'T ANYMORE

A young lady came into the store looking for a Rhody Rugger
A Rhody Rugger FROM THE STORE?
A Rhody Rugger she wanted, our hooker she got
I DON'T WORK THERE ANYMORE!

Many other songs were also a major part of these sometimes sophomoric rugby parties. Some of the more traditional songs are listed below but it didn't matter if you had a great voice or not – everybody sang these rugby songs with the wild lyrics and the beer made it all good! I left out the more vulgar songs and there were some of these at the predominately male attended rugby parties. Political correctness did not exist during our rugby years but we did not write these "unique" songs – they were handed down to rugby teams over the years and they were quite old.

The Wild Rover

I've been a wild rover for many a year,
And I've spent all my money on whiskey and beer
But now I'm returning with gold in great store,
And never will play the wild rover no more

Chorus:
And it's no, nay, never!
No, nay, never, no more,
Will I play the wild rover?
No never, no more

I went to an ale house I used to frequent,
And I told the landlady my money was spent
I asked her for credit, she answered me nay,
Such custom like yours I can get any day

Chorus

I took from my pocket ten sovereigns bright,
And the landlady's eyes opened wide with delight
She said, "I have whiskeys and wines of the best,
And I'll take you upstairs, and I'll show you the rest"

Chorus

I'll go home to my parents, confess what I've done,

And I'll ask them to pardon their prodigal son

And if they caress me as oft times before,

I never will play the wild rover no more!

Be Kind to Your Web-footed Friends – sung to the tune of *Stars and Stripes Forever*

Be kind to your web-footed friends

For a duck may be somebody's mother

Be kind to your friends in the swamp

Where the weather is cool and damp

Now you may think that this is the end

Well it is...

Swing Low Sweet Chariot

Chorus:

Swing low, sweet chariot

Coming for to carry me home

Swing low, sweet chariot

Coming for to carry me home

I looked over Jordan, and what did I see?

(Coming for to carry me home)

I saw a band of angels coming after me

(Coming for to carry me home)

Chorus

If you get back to heaven before I do

(Coming for to carry me home)

You'll tell all my friends, I'll be coming there too

(Coming for to carry me home)

Note: These two verses of the song are done first with just singing, then singing with actions, then humming with actions, then a silent version with actions only.

Lumberjack Song

I'm a lumberjack and I'm OK,

I sleep all night and I work all day.

He's a lumberjack and he's OK,

He sleeps all night and works all day.

I cut down trees, I eat my lunch,

I go to the lavatory.

On Wednesdays I go shopping,

And have buttered scones for tea.

I'm a lumberjack and I'm OK,

I sleep all night and I work all day.

More verses, etc…………………………..

He's a lumberjack and he's OK,

He sleeps all night and works all day.

I cut down trees, I skip and jump,

I like to press wild flowers,

I put on women's clothing,

And hang around in bars.

He cuts down trees, he skips and jumps,

He likes to press wild flowers,

He put on women's clothing,

And hang around in bars.

I'm a lumberjack and I'm OK,

I sleep all night and I work all day.

He's a lumberjack and he's OK,

He sleeps all night and works all day.

I cut down trees, I wear high heels,

Suspenders and a bra,

I wish I were a girlie,

Just like my dear papa.

More verses, etc............

Why Are We Waiting? – sung to the tune of *Oh, Come All Ye Faithful*

Why are we waiting?

Why are we waiting?

Oh, why are we waiting?

Oh why, why, why?

Why are we waiting?

Why are we waiting?

Oh, why are we waiting?

Oh, why are we waiting?

Oh, why are we waiting?

Oh why, why, why?

(Repeat until the beer arrives)

Note: "clean" version for "mixed company"

In Dublin's fair city,

Where the girls are so pretty,

I first set my eyes on sweet Molly Malone,

As she wheels her wheel barrow,

Thro' streets broad and narrow,

Crying Cockles and Mussels Alive, alive O!

(Chorus)

Alive, alive O! Alive, alive O,

Crying Cockles and Mussels Alive, alive O!

She was a fishmonger,

But sure 'twas no wonder,

For so were her father and mother before,

And they each wheels their barrow,

Thro' streets broad and narrow,

Crying Cockles and Mussels Alive, alive O!

(Repeat Chorus)

She died of a fever,

And no one could save her,

And that was the end of sweet Molly Malone,

But her ghost wheels her barrow,

Thro' streets broad and narrow,

Crying Cockles and Mussels Alive, alive O!

(Repeat Chorus)

Why was he born so beautiful?

Why was he born at all?

He's no f......... use to anyone,

He's no f......... use at all,

He should be publicly peed on,

He should be publicly shot (bang, bang),

He should be tied to a urinal,

And left there to fester and rot.

So, DRINK chug-a-lug,

Drink chug-a-lug,

Drink chug-a-lug,

DRINK!

Ireland's Call

Come the day and come the hour

Come the power and the glory!

We have come to answer

Our Country's call

From the four proud provinces of Ireland!

CHORUS:

Ireland, Ireland

Together standing tall

Shoulder to shoulder

We'll answer Ireland's call!

From the mighty Glens of Antrim

From the rugged hills of Galway!

From the walls of Limerick

And Dublin Bay

From the four proud provinces of Ireland!

CHORUS

Hearts of steel

And heads unbowing

Vowing never to be broken

We will fight, until

We can fight no more

From the four proud provinces of Ireland!

CHORUS

Ireland, Ireland

Together standing tall

Shoulder to shoulder

We'll answer Ireland's call!

We'll answer Ireland's call!

If I Were the Marrying Kind – also called "The Rugby Song"

If I were the marrying kind

Which thank the lord I'm not, sir

The kind of rugger I would wed

Would be a Rugby.....

(The team points to the hooker.

The hooker puts a beer on top of his head.)

HOOKER: Hooker sir!

GROUP: Why sir?

HOOKER:

'cause I'd swipe balls, and you'd swipe balls

We'd all swipe balls together
We'd be alright in the middle of the night
Swiping balls together
GROUP:
If I were the marrying kind
Which thank the lord I'm not, sir
the kind of rugger I would wed
would be a Rugby .....
(The team points to the props. The Props put beers on their head.)
PROPS: Prop sir!
GROUP: Why sir?

PROPS:
'cause I'd support a hooker
and you'd support a hooker
We'd all support a hooker together
We'd be alright in the middle of the night
supporting hookers together

Note: There are many more verses for each rugby position or pitch term and some are "R" rated.

I Don't Want to Join the Army

I don't want to join the army
Oh, I don't want to be a soldier
I don't want to join the fightin' class
I just want to go
Down to old Soho
Pinchin' all the girlies in the shoulder blades
Oh, I don't want to see the Queen's dominions
Why London's full o' girls I've never 'ad

I just want to stay in England

Jolly jolly England

And follow in the footsteps of me dad

So call out the members of the Queen's Marines

Call out the King's Artillery

Call out me mother

Me sister and me brother

But for Chrissake don't call me

Monday night me 'and was on her ankle

Tuesday night me 'and was on her knees

Wednesday night, success!

I lifted up her dress

Thursday night I lifted up her silk chemise

Well, Friday night I got me 'and talking about it

Saturday night I gave her just a tweak

Sunday after supper

I finally made it with her

And now I'm payin' thirty bob a week (Gorblimey...)

Note: A few words I changed to make it "cleaner".

Dough, A Thing I Buy Beer With – sung to the tune of – *Doe a deer* from "The Sound of Music."

Dough a Thing I Buy Beer With

Ray a guy who buys me beer

Me, a guy I buy beer for

Fa, a long way to the bar

So, I think I'll have a beer

La, la la la la la la

Tea, no thanks I'll have a beer

That brings us back to dough oh oh oh...

Below are two articles from the "Cigar". The second article appeared a few days after the first match summary article appeared. The student newspaper was published twice a week.
Cortland State whom we trounced by a score of 64 to 6 had behaved quite badly at the post party and the URI Rugby Club sent the "Cigar" a disclaimer and our apologies. We were indeed gentlemen.

Rugby club rolls, sweeps Cortland

Coming off last week's stunning victory over, Brown, a perennial New England powerhouse, the URI rugby club kept on its winning ways by trouncing Cortland State by a score of 64-6 Saturday at the Keaney fields.

Rhody also took the "B" and "C" games by identical 20-4 scores in turning another successful sweep for the ruggers.

In the "A" game, Rhody completely dominated play. When the dust had subsided the ruggers had totalled an amazing 64 points on 15 tries and 2 conversions, against a single try and conversion for Cortland.

Cortland rugby

To the Cigar:

"On behalf of the URI Rugby team, I apologize to the "Concerned Students of Bressler, 2 N" and any other students affected by the rudeness of the Cortland Rugby Team.

I've heard reports on their behavior from all corners of the campus; from dancing on tables in the Pub to harassing the girls of Delta Zeta, Bressler, Coddington and the list goes on.

It is now apparent, Cortland came to Rhode Island to party as, as the score on and off the field reflects. Our team has decided in view of the above incidents that we will no longer play Cortland. I am sorry for all the nonsense and inconvience Cortland imposed on the campus.

Below are a few casual photos after some matches when many were looking forward to the post match party. Kent Chase with a friend is in the top left photo; he was always joking and smiling. In the right photo are best buds Harry Westler and Rob – a deadly scrum-half and fly-half combination for any URI opponent. (Photos by G. Desisto and R. Reynolds)

Ethan Wise in the bottom left photo, a pack player with good speed who played with the sevens teams is posing for the camera with Reed – one of Rhody's great wingers. In the right photo, the young girl on the far left is our unofficial team photographer – Gail Desisto and two of her friends.

We must have lost this match – Rich "Tats" Tattier and Mike T look quite depressed in this photo as they drink a pint or two from paper cups on the sideline.

Below at a different match – Nick Weston looks so serious and Rob is smiling next to John Hoder from the Providence RFC who seems to be in street clothes but also smiling for the camera. (Both photos by L. O'Neil)

CHAPTER 4

"Spiderman"

"I went to college. I had a double major in biology and physical education, but my major was wrestling."

Dan Gable – Retired All-American college wrestler, Olympic Gold Medal winner, and legendary coach.

September 1978 – an elementary school, Providence Rhode Island

Growing up, I always enjoyed hanging out and playing with my brother's and sister's young children and that's why I majored in Elementary Education at the University of Rhode Island when I was enrolled. I minored in English because I happened to take more than a few English classes in my first two years of college so this fit my curriculum requirements and I would be able to graduate in four years. I also took these classes because I thought Poetry, Short Stories, and Italian Literature would not be difficult classes and I could build up my low overall cume that I had obtained as a freshman and sophomore student. I enjoyed living on campus and away from home during my college years but I really enjoyed the social aspect of college rather than school work. My grades were impacted in those early semesters because I lived in a fraternity where I enjoyed many of their parties as well as some of the campus-wide events, concerts, and other social activities.

In the mid-nineties, this fraternity and a few of the other fraternities that were located on one of the main roads at the top of the campus were forced to move off campus and their lease ended due to their inappropriate behavior and bill payment neglect. These older fraternity buildings that were not in very good condition due to lack of maintenance and age were later torn down.

This location at the top of the campus situated close to the "Quad" never looked better now with all the new buildings built there and utilized by the university for other URI housing and departments. My fraternity's land was reallocated to a private company. This company called "The Foundation" helps raise money for URI which is badly needed now that the state has cut much more aid from the state school's budget over the last few years.

During college, I played rugby, hung out with my Sigma Nu fraternity brothers and ruggers, played pickup basketball, and visited the local campus pub (It was actually called "The Pub".) between all the difficult class work. I sometimes put school and grades at a lower priority than it should have been. Now after graduation, I needed to find a full-time job with benefits and to find out if the classes I took in school would help me survive working in the "real" world.

I didn't have many job interviews that first year after graduation and I didn't have a single job offer and very few teaching interviews. Luckily, one of my rugby teammates Harry worked in the Housing and Residential Life Office at URI as a graduate student and they needed a few part-time employees for various job duties so he offered me a position. It worked out for both parties. I was paid an hourly rate with no benefits for a temporary position that consisted of two different jobs and I worked about 35 hours per week.

I then continued playing rugby for the University of Rhode Island and worked on campus moving furniture during the day and helping out as a substitute evening manager at night in the dorms. I particularly enjoyed working in the "all girls" freshman dorms during that year – that's where I first noticed my wife Jeannie who was a freshman in Merrow Hall. I didn't meet her until a Spring Break rugby match that our team scheduled in Florida during that same year. I couldn't tell you the college we played against in Florida for that early evening match but I remember we had many Rhody fans at the match. The free kegs of beer on the sidelines might have contributed to the abnormally large attendance away from our home field. We won the match, and Jeannie and I met again at a campus party and started dating; so rugby even played a large part in my marriage and the birth of my two children – Sean and Casey.

The following year, I was interviewed at the end of August at a Catholic school in Providence and I accepted that position. I guess they were desperate due to the low pay scale that Catholic schools were associated with in those years – and very few applied for this teaching job. Also, one of the parochial nuns who worked in the school was friendly with my Aunt Rita, also a nun, who taught Library Studies in a Catholic school in East Providence. The pay for this nine-month teaching position was six thousand and eight hundred dollars. Public schools at that time paid double that amount. I was a steal no matter what anybody thought of my minimal employment history.

It was the first day of school for all the young students at this Catholic school where I was working back in 1978 and this was my first year of teaching. I was assigned the fourth grade for this class's regular subjects, fifth and sixth grade for History, and fifth and sixth grade for Physical Education. I was very nervous – I had no previous teacher experience including no substitute teaching or much hands-on actual classroom work during my four years at URI.

My practical teaching experience other than book and writing assignments was one student teaching semester and that consisted of teaching a first grade class with young children not much past the baby level. The letter "T" was one example of an entire lesson plan for this age level. This did not prepare me at all for my first year of "production" teaching with older children. I was so nervous that I introduced myself to another teacher that first day of school as "Mr. Murphy".

The school was quite diverse in ethnicity and economics. Children who attended this school consisted of local kids from the neighborhood, children in a lower financial end of the spectrum who lived in older areas that surrounded the outskirts of the school, and some children from upper class sections in nearby cities and towns who were dropped off by their parents each day. This school had an excellent reputation for discipline and education. It consisted mostly of lay teachers like myself and a few parochial nuns who taught religion and special education only. The principal was also a nun and she ruled with an iron fist.

Right away, I think most of the young children liked me even though I was clueless on how to handle or teach children at this time in my first full-time teaching assignment. One day, one of the students approached me as I came into school after surviving the first week or two. First, he asked me if he could carry my milk crate for me. Instead of a nice book bag or an appropriate book carrier, I carried my books, notebooks, and lunch in a "Monroe Dairy" official dark blue milk crate that I had used for various other purposes during college.

Bottles of milk used to be delivered to families' doorsteps by "Milk Men" who worked for various dairy companies such as "Monroe Dairy" out of Rhode Island when I was a child and these plastic or metal milk containers held their share of the bottles of milk they brought to the families. Some companies still deliver milk to families but over the years, home milk delivery dwindled and many of these "Milk Men" became obsolete but the milk crates survived. I also wore a bright "Keaney Blue" windbreaker jacket with the large letters – "Rhode Island Rugby Club" on the back of this jacket. I must have been quite a sight for most of the veteran teachers.

Frank Keaney was a legendary coach, teacher, and mentor at **Rhode Island State, the local Rhode Island college in the 1920s through the late 1940s** who created the school's athletic team color – a bright, light blue. He was also a chemistry professor for over ten years. This color is similar to North Carolina's special blue school color. Years later, Rhode Island State's name was changed to the University of Rhode Island.

Keaney was credited with revolutionizing college basketball by devising the fast break in the 1930s and for turning the Rhode Island basketball team into a national basketball powerhouse in the thirties and forties when the NIT (National Invitational Tournament) was the major national college basketball championship. I hope we can reach that same level again with URI's latest basketball coach – Dan Hurley.

"Mr. Murphy," little Gary told me that day, he was in my fourth grade class, "I think everybody in this neighborhood must like you because your car hasn't been stolen yet." He was not joking, it was an inner city school in a decent neighborhood but some crime and poverty did exist. I grew up in suburbia so this would also be another obstacle for me to face during this upcoming school year.

Many of the teachers tried to help me out during this rough year but there was one woman whom I knew from some of the same classes I attended at URI who seemed to be somewhat annoyed with me. I'm not sure what her problem with me was but she didn't let up giving me a hard time during that year. I think she was jealous that many of her children in some of her classes seemed to enjoy my unorthodox and unorganized method of teaching and I did let some of her children get away with certain things she wouldn't let them get away with. I picked my battles with students to avoid more issues than I could handle. It reached its climax only a few months into the school year after she confronted me with a drawing I created for some of the children in her regular class but who attended my history class.

Motivation seemed to be lacking with some of the children in my classes which then turned into discipline problems and a few major class disturbances. The one major rule or tool I remember from college course work that was supposed to help with discipline problems was – ignore undesired behavior and reinforce good behavior with positive rewards such as gold stars, free time, praise, etc. I was a very good cartoon illustrator when I was younger and I never lost this artistic skill but it was limited. If you told me to draw a dog, I would draw a dog that looked like a first grader drew it, stick figure like. If I drew a dog while looking at a cartoon character of a dog such as Marmaduke from the cartoon strip found in many newspapers, I could reproduce it exactly.

On weekends, I made sure I drew a few cartoons in pencil on plain white paper and only handed them out to the well-behaved children who completed their work. The kids really enjoyed coloring these homemade drawings of some of their favorite cartoon characters and some of the kids would even try to reproduce my drawings using pencil or markers. It was a big hit.

On a late Monday afternoon, I was greeted by this co-teacher who was holding one of my more elaborate "Spiderman" drawings that displayed Spiderman the super hero with a very intricate, detailed web pattern costume that he wore; flying through the air clinging to a large, fine spider web.

"You are a liar, Connor!" she yelled at me. "OK," I replied. "What's going on today, Linda?" "Why do you lie to the children?" she said to me. I had no idea what she was talking about but this was not good. "Did you draw this?" she responded. I think I knew where this was going now, I thought to myself. Linda was also the Art teacher in the school and evidently, I outdid some of her work with this recent drawing. "I did not draw that exact drawing, I made many copies of a drawing and that is one of them. The original is on my desk." "If you could draw like this, you would be the Art teacher!" she replied. I walked away from her and went back to my classroom.

There were a few other early incidents that confirmed I was a first year novice teacher at this school such as the time that I forgot a school choir practice for an upcoming special religious celebration in the church that was located across the street from the school. I was teaching my fourth grade class a lesson in history late in the afternoon when I noticed it was particularly quiet outside my classroom. I opened the door and stepped outside into the hallway. Nobody was in the hallway and there were no students or teachers in the classroom right next to mine. I quickly had my students form a line and we marched over to the church. "Glad you could make it, Mr. Murphy." Sister Elizabeth the school principal greeted me as we arrived. More than a few soft laughs were heard in the previously very quiet church after her satirical comment.

The other incident occurred during recess when one of my toughest fourth grade students abruptly left the schoolyard and ran down the street. I had no idea what to do or where he was going but I ran after him and had to physically carry him back to the school. I forget what the Principal told me I should have done but I knew I couldn't lose a student during my first few weeks at the school and this could affect my next teaching assignment if this one didn't work out.

I did survive that "teaching" year but a few times, I needed help from my rugby teammates with grading daily paper assignments, small projects, or homework when I fell behind in this important paperwork. When I needed to make a second practice for an upcoming important match, they gladly came to my rescue. They were fast learners and had better penmanship than me so I had to have them scribble a little when writing some of their comments and assigning grades on the papers or projects they corrected to match my signature. I did double-check the major project work.

The first drawing below was a cartoon I created before the first Providence RFC "A" match that we played on their home field. This could have backfired on me. I passed out many of these flyers to all of our players a few days prior to the match but somebody delivered one to a Providence rugger so most of their team saw this negative cartoon picture. I'm sure Bob Hoder, the captain of the team, and Bob Cagney who played with us for one season who later played for Providence had a few words for their team before they took to the rugby field on Saturday and my name was mentioned.

I learned about this unknown traitor after the match from some of the Providence ruggers. We beat them pretty good that day and I can't remember anyone trying to take me out with a dirty tackle or any of their team playing very dirty against us. The URI pack had a great game and our backs scored a few easy tries. I added the literal "We" to this cartoon after the match and saved one copy. I came up with this pre-game little joke when I found a rugby cartoon in a magazine (There was no Internet back then.) and made some minor changes to it. My artistic talent only consists of drawing reproductions of other cartoons – my brain works like a copying machine.

The second drawing below is an original cartoon depicting Rhody the URI Ram mascot in karate attire that my daughter created for me one recent Father's Day. She can draw anything without looking at the object; a talent not inherited from my wife or me. My son inherited my analytical work skills and my stubbornness but definitely not my height – he grew to be six feet four.

CHAPTER 5

Happy hour practices

"If you train hard, you'll not only be hard, you'll be hard to beat."

Herschel Walker – Retired American professional football great who played in the USFL and NFL and was an Olympic bobsledder.

Rugby practices and matches were held behind the "Keaney" gymnasium on various grass fields that the school designated for the Rhode Island Rugby Club and each year we seemed to be assigned to a new location. We also were given a specific date that we had to abide by at the beginning of the spring season practice sessions. If we had a long winter and the field was still soft and soggy, we could not practice on our own field. Instead, we would search for any open area we could play on such as an empty parking lot or any field on the outskirts of campus that had a barren surface of grass or dirt that we could train on. Other times, we would sneak on these practice fields before the allotted date and hoped nobody working in the Athletic department noticed us.

I remember after one long winter, our first few practices were on a side parking lot next to a deserted area near one of the gymnasium buildings. I was working construction that year and I forgot my sneakers and we couldn't wear spikes on tar so there I was working on rugby fundamentals and drills wearing heavy work boots. At one point, some of the players got bored so we played a short game of two-hand touch with two full sides of fifteen players against each other. I broke one long run for a try beating the wing and centers of the opposing team (mostly "B" players) and many of the veterans had a small chuckle out of seeing me sprinting down the asphalt "field" in a dirty white t-shirt and the clunky work boots I wore that day.

These practices were very simple especially at the beginning of my playing career at URI because we coached ourselves for the most part and didn't know all of the rules or many practice fundamentals and plays. We did hook up with some "coaches" (ruggers who had more match experience than the rest of us) from time to time who were graduate students who might have played the game at their previous school, and one of the local rugby legends in the state – Bob Hoder. Bob played in the pack for the Providence RFC and also coached the team. Hoder owns a rugby retail store in East Providence that supplied many high schools, colleges, and men's teams as well as our team with rugby jerseys, shorts, and other gear.

The Barrington, Rhode Island native had a very good college football career playing for URI and was captain of the team in the early sixties and he played semi-professional football for the Providence Rhode Island Steamrollers after he graduated. He is also a member of the URI Athletic Hall of Fame, inducted in 1994.

Bob is the only rugby player that I saw ejected or thrown out of a rugby match. The referee threw him out of the match after a long heated argument between Bob and an opposing player that occurred and some punches were thrown. But the final straw was when the player continued to harass Bob with some unpleasant short sentences and Bob spit in the rugger's face – directly in front of the referee who was trying to stop the ruckus. That's how I remember it, but Bob may have a different version of this event. Bob didn't take crap from anybody. At the time, I was playing wing for Providence and both Bob and his brother John who also played in the scrum were key players, officers of the club, and spokesmen for this team and the game itself.

Years later, Bob also coached high school rugby including Barrington High School in Rhode Island and this team won five New England championships. Bob helped us by attending some of our practices from time to time and explaining to us what we needed to work on or improve upon and provided our team with some new drills or plays. These short sessions definitely allowed us to elevate our game and also helped Bob's own team. At these meetings, he secretly recruited many of the better URI ruggers over the years for his own men's club who after graduation left the URI club team and played for Providence. I was not one of those players – I competed for another three years with URI after graduating and living in the area.

I graduated in four years with a BA degree in Education but continued playing for URI because I still had younger friends who were on the team and had not graduated yet. I spanned many years and many seasons because I had difficulty obtaining a full-time professional job (I was a teacher for one of those years.) and I really didn't want to work full time at that point in my life. I was still enjoying college life but not taking classes – it was a great social time that I knew would end when I found the right job and started working a forty-hour week. I enjoyed the South County area – close to the beaches and I had much to do in the summer surrounded by young people all the time.

I frequently called my mom, at least once a week and checked in with her to see how both my mom and dad were doing. In those days, health care was cheap and I lived on a small paycheck that could cover my old cars, (I owned a 1969 Chevy Nova until this car broke down and then I owned a 1972 Ford Pinto.) insurance, food, and rent. It was fun continuing playing sports and having no real responsibility back then, still hanging out on campus and at the local school pub. My mom actually contributed to my laziness by financing my monthly college loan payments. It wasn't a very large amount but my parents didn't have any extra money, both worked jobs that didn't pay well. This was very special to me even though at that time, I didn't realize it.

I sent my mom a few letters seen below (no email or personal computers then) during my first full year of playing rugby, with some of the "Cigar" articles about the team. My mom and dad did catch one of my away matches – against Brown University in the pouring rain and a muddied pitch. We lost in a slugfest. Harry was at his "best" and had many great hits and tackles. After the match, my dad asked – "Who was that guy?"

Mom,

I thought you might like this article that was in the school paper. They make us sound pretty good. I'll probably be home next weekend. See you then. Hi Dad.

Mom + Dad,

My picture was in the school paper last week, so I saved you a copy. You should be able to pick me out. They caught me at a good time, I was just standing there. So much for a crazy game.

Around that time I started attending karate classes across the street from a fine drinking establishment that many of the URI college students frequented – "Twin Willows". This restaurant and bar still exists today but now, it is much more family friendly. In the fifties and early sixties, it was a small pub and piano bar where many adults and older URI students, professors, and graduate students visited. In the early seventies – when the drinking age was lowered – it turned into a busy college environment with few adults, especially on weekends when the URI pub was designated mostly for date nights. It was at the end of my third year out of school and I had recently quit the construction job I was working at when my mom questioned my work ethics during one of those weekly phone calls. **"Connor, are you going to come home someday and get a real job and stop playing games?"** That was the only time my mom ever questioned my slacker lifestyle and that following fall, I did move home and registered for a few computer classes at the local state community college. "Data Processing" was what it was called back then, many years before the Internet and home computers. It became my new career for the next thirty years and more.

Our practices started with an "Indian" run. I'm not sure who thought of this drill and how it was named but this is what an "Indian" run warm-up consisted of – as explained in the following paragraph. (Today I think it is called "single file" or "last man" run.)

Every team member would line up one behind the other on the practice pitch and begin jogging in line as the line moved forward around the pitch. Then one player at the end of the row would run as fast as they could towards the front of the group. Next, the player with the rugby ball (We always incorporated the rugby ball with any drill we worked on.) at the head of the line would pass the ball back to this sprinting rugger right before he reached the beginning of the line. The next player at the end of the line would then do the same, race up to the front of the line and receive a backwards pass from that new rugger at the head of the line. This went on until each rugger fielded four or five passes depending upon how many ruggers were at practice that afternoon.

After this warm-up exercise, the team would separate into backs and forwards and one of the captains of our team or a senior player would explain a drill or two that everybody would then work on. I guess we also practiced some plays but I don't remember many of these organized plays because I played wing, and wings were the last players to receive the ball so at that point, options were limited as opposed to the inside backs' options and opportunities, who consistently battled in the middle of the pitch during matches.

If the drills didn't go well or if some of the team members were not listening and goofing off (As I said we coached ourselves and players coaching other players could be difficult.), one of the captains, especially Rob, would stop the practice and just tell all of us, "That's it, we're scrimmaging!" or "All right, let's go Live!" Most of the team who were ex-football players seemed to enjoy scrimmages better than some of the boring practice drills. At times, competition between the "A" team ruggers and "B" team ruggers was so serious that our team scrimmages were tougher than our regular Saturday matches and injuries were common. I think that's how we actually became better players – scrimmaging hard against each other. **The strong and fast survived these battles.**

Practices also determined who was going to play on the designated teams the upcoming Saturday and everybody wanted to play on the "A" team. A selection team made up of captains and veteran "A" team players would vote on the teams after the Friday practice. Friday's practices were usually very light practices if any practice at all. Sometimes, we played Frisbee or just jogged around the rugby field and stretched our legs.

We had very few team rules for the Rhody Rugby Club but you had to attend at least two practices during the week to be considered for the "A" team. A few of the players who had difficult majors or who lived off campus made sure they made the Friday practice even if they showed up after practice and joined the team at the local campus pub "Happy Hour" that officially started at 4:30 in the afternoon. This would count as one official practice but this really applied to the veteran, definite "A" team players only and I don't think any rugger ever questioned this vague policy or rule.

I had some of my better matches on Saturday when I stayed too long at this Friday only event, sometimes never leaving until closing time. Happy Hour was more than one hour for many of the Rhody Ruggers. I did say we had fun, pitchers of "fun" as many of the ruggers called the Pub's pitchers of beer.

Sometimes, if Happy Hour was boring I would leave early and head back to my fraternity house and strip down to my boxer shorts, socks, and green high top Converse sneakers and race cars that drove by on Upper College Road – an early evening workout. This was probably not a great thing to do the night before a match.

Drinking at the campus pub also helped us tweak some of our rugby party "stupid rugger" tricks, which were very similar to the late night television host David Letterman's famous "stupid human" tricks. This was the place where some of us would practice our "tricks" or "gimmicks" in preparation for the upcoming postgame party. During the postgame parties, players from either team could perform a funny, outrageous, or just plain dumb "trick" and try to outdo the opposing team's "antics".

A few examples of these ad hoc or practiced tricks that the URI Rugby Team performed were: drinking beer through your nose, drinking beer through your jersey while it was pulled over your head, (This was similar to the unknown comic's actions on "The Gong Show" – an older comedy, television game show that you might have watched if you are close to my age.), lighting parts of your body on fire (This was one of my specialties – please don't try this at home!), breaking beer glasses with your teeth, jumping though one of your own legs held knee high across your waist while standing on the other leg, swallowing live earth worms, balancing various foreign objects on your head, etc. They all seemed funny at the time after a few pints of beer but made no sense to many of the fans or non-rugby athletes.

The photo below was taken prior to one of our home matches in the spring (fifteens). "Sid" the dog was our only mascot. I am the third rugger from the left, bottom row. Barry R and Rob are next to me on my right.
(Photo by Yearbook staff)

The photos below were taken before and after some of our New York Sevens tournament matches. It was always cold on Randall's Island in late November. (Photos by G. Desisto)

The photo below was taken during a "B" team home match. Ted Kiley is the fly-half starting the offensive play after the ball came out from a scrum. Dave Jenks and "E", URI forwards are releasing from the scrum and starting to chase the play. Rob in a hooded sweatshirt and a whistle refereed this match.
Was this legal?
(Photo by Yearbook staff)

Mike T in the top left photo below is making his move while I watch which direction he goes. Nick and "Tats" are in front of Mike. Dan Saladar in the right photo is preparing to punt the ball. Rob and Jake Knowles are seen breaking some hard tackles in the two bottom photos. (Photos by Yearbook staff)

I really like this photo that seems to show only the URI pack and our opponent with no backs in sight. (Photo by Yearbook staff)

More action photos below left – a high throw-in from the sideline during an "A" match. Bob Hoder refereed this match – he is seen behind Lenny Thibodeau, the second URI rugger on the left. (Photo by Yearbook staff)

Another throw-in action photo above right close up with an unidentified Rhody Rugger ready to haul in the ball at its apex. (Photo by Yearbook staff)

The photo below shows the diehard URI ruggers after one of the Providence matches. We were still partying on the sidelines very late after the win. Check out the various warm-ups and jackets. I'm the fifth rugger from the left. (Photo by G. Desisto)

Reed and Gail are pictured in the photo below after a loss at one of the New England Rugby Union Tournaments that featured the best men's teams in this area. Gary "Dish" Famelly who was injured that day is in the background. We did lose our share of URI matches over the years but these losses helped the team get stronger. (Photo by L. O'Neil)

This photo shows Barry and I after losing to a touring English men's select side – the Northampton RFC when we both played wing for the New England Rugby Select Side. Tryouts for this predominantly men's club select team was by invitation only and this also proved that: URI Rugby had made – "The Big Time". We lost 10 to 9 in that special match so I don't know what I'm smiling about. Neither one of us received the ball much that day. Many of the select/ all-star teams that some of the Rhode Island ruggers tried out for or played on relied on much scrum possession and kicking – not our style of play.
(Photo by L. O'Neil)

Below – a page from the Northampton RFC team's program guide – the team that Barry and I played against in May, 1979. They had quite a history behind them especially compared to the Rhode Island Rugby Club, comprised of students who coached themselves, and that was founded in 1966. Northampton RFC was founded in 1879.

Your visitors

Northampton Football Club was founded during the 1879-80 season and this tour marks the start of its Centenary celebrations. In its early days it was a section of a youth club attached to St. James' Church, Northampton when it acquired the nickname of "The Saints" which has remained with it throughout its history. Since 1891 it has played at Franklin's Gardens, Northampton, an attractive ground with excellent facilities which the Club purchased in 1977.

Early this century the Club established itself as one of the major Rugby Union clubs in the United Kingdom with regular fixtures against the leading clubs in England and Wales. Indeed, in the 1975-76 season it was top of the English Rugby Clubs Merit Table and of the Anglo-Welsh Merit Table and was presented with trophies by the two national newspapers which compiled those tables.

Over the years its players have won more than 250 International honours or "caps" and Northampton players have captained the England XV on many occasions. The Club has one prop forward in the current England XV and one in the England Under 23 XV. One of its former International players is Frank Sykes who is well known to rugby enthusiasts in the U.S.A.

The Club is fortunate in having on its committee a number of men who have played important roles in English rugby over many years. Don White (our President) and Ron Jacobs, both of whom wore an England shirt for many years are also on the Committee of the Rugby Football Union and with David Powell and Bob Taylor, both England and British Lion players, continue to give the benefit of their experience to the Club.

The Club last toured in the U.S.A. in 1973, playing matches in Indianapolis, Champaign-Urbana, Madison, Wisconsin, Chicago and Ann Arbor.

Our acknowledgements

Northampton Football Club and the Tour Party wish to record their sincere and grateful thanks to: —

Our American friends who so admirably made the arrangements in the U.S.A.

One of our game attraction flyers for a Friday night match we sometimes played under the lights on the football or soccer practice field. This brought the crowds. Twice, we played three rugby matches in one week including a night match. That was rough on the body!

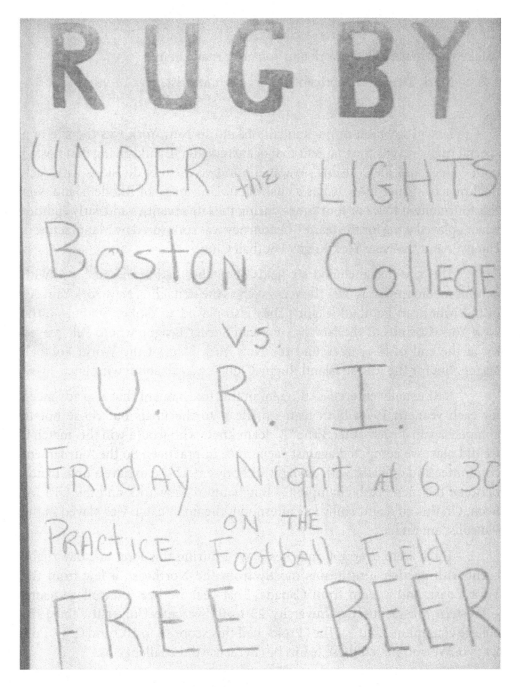

CHAPTER 6

New York sevens tournament

"Make your mark in New York and you are a made man."

Mark Twain – American author and humorist.

Downing Stadium on Randall's Island in New York was the site of a special rugby sevens tournament that occurred after Thanksgiving that hosted both college and men's teams separated into two distinct divisions with each final match winner crowned as a champion. University of Rhode Island won this tournament three or four times during the late seventies and early eighties when I played wing for the team. The tourney was sponsored by Manufacturers Hanover and the New York Rugby Football Club.

This site that included six fields or pitches had been associated with various mediocre teams over the years such as the struggling New York Yankees of the American Football league (They also played at Yankee Stadium.), the New York Cosmos of the North American Soccer League whom Pele played for at the end of his career, and the New York Stars of the World Football league. But for the Rhode Island Rugby Club, it was all about winning.

URI usually entered a "B" team in this tournament that also advanced far each year. In 1978, both teams made it to the finals but chose not to compete against each other. (The "B" team knew who would win this match if we did play; we competed against each other in practice.) So the tournament committee and officials, with daylight still present, chose to have a final match between the men's club champion – Binghamton New York and the URI "A" team. On this cold and chilly late afternoon, the final match was played in the old coliseum arena.

There were over 150 matches played during this long one day rugby event with participating teams mostly from the Northeast, a few from the West Coast, and a team from Canada. That year we beat the college teams – Western Massachusetts University 22 to 0, Syracuse University, the 1976 college champion 12 to 3, (The "Projo" had this score 16 to 10.) and C. W. Post 24 to 0. We dominated these teams but Syracuse did challenge us.

I remember warming up and trying to stay warm in the old, dilapidated bathrooms of this stadium before the final match. Rugby matches seemed to be held on out of the way fields, and bathrooms and showers were never close to the playing area, if they even existed. Luckily, woods covered the outskirts of many of these pitch locations and that's where we took care of business. Showers after a match might have taken place at our home field battles before the traditional postgame parties but at away matches, hardly ever and I doubt the showers worked on Randall's Island. I know I was so cold I didn't bother to check them out in the dark after this finals match ended.

Dressed in heavy jackets, winter hats, winter gloves, and various sweats, we tried to stretch our legs and prepare for this final men's club match. None of us wore the same warm-up outfits during these early playing days and on this cold day, it was no different. Some of my teammates wore their high school gear, some wore generic sweat pants and hooded sweatshirts, but I usually wore loose military fatigue pants (I joined a Marine ROTC program with a fraternity brother and good friend – Chip Fales – during my sophomore year and owned a few pair of these military pants.) or old, ragged "painter" blue jeans, and any jacket or hooded sweatshirt I found in my closet. Years later, the team did buy official rugby jackets from Hoder's store – "Rugby Imports" with our school name on the back and designed by Rob. Many of us wore these jackets to the matches after this large purchase and this made us look more like a "real" rugby club.

We were huddled close together sitting on the cold tile floor preparing for this final match that many of us didn't even want to play due to the cold weather, the late start of the match, and too much downtime between our last college match and the final "finals". Rugby is a contact sport and each match you play in sevens means more bumps and bruises and little time to heal compared to fifteen-a-side matches in the regular season – one match on one day.

The match was a tough defensive battle with little scoring. I remember making a tackle early in the match and I took a hard shot to my nose. I thought it hurt more due to the cold weather and I didn't think much about it until I looked in the mirror after the long ride home while taking a shower. It still hurt and was quite swollen. I think I had a small break but being born with the typical Irish flat, pug nose, it didn't look much different than my original nose structure. This was the last match of the season, so it didn't matter – no more rugby meant no more injuries and I didn't have to play the next match with a slightly broken nose. It was five months away until the next season and the next rugby match or game.

Rhody took a 6-0 lead in the first half on a nice run by Mike T, our scrum-half in this final match. A penalty kick by Binghamton made it a 6 to 3 close game with one half to go. Both teams must have been frozen solid during the last, very cold 7 minutes and Reed scored the only try in that second half and Rob made both two point conversion kicks.

The whistle blew at the end of the match and URI beat Binghamton RFC with a score of 12 to 3. A college rugby team beating a men's rugby club in the special finals must have surprised many teams that day especially the better men's teams who lost to Binghamton earlier that day. The next year and subsequent years – college team champions were never challenged by the men's championship teams and the two distinct divisions never overlapped.

Rhody ruggers win tourney

Special to the Journal-Bulletin

NEW YORK — The University of Rhode Island A team was the surprise winner of the annual Manufacturers Hanover New York Sevens Rugby Tournament held yesterday at Downing Stadium, Randall's Island.

Rhode Island defeated Binghamton, N.Y., 12-3, in the championship game. The matches, featuring seven players per side, were each 15 minutes long.

Rhode Island had gained the final with a 16-10 victory over Syracuse.

There were 150 matches played in the day-long event with teams coming from all over the Northeast, as well as California, Illinois and Canada.

In the 1979 New York Sevens Rugby Tournament, URI won again for the third straight year. In this college only tournament the "B" team lost to Central Connecticut State by a score of 18 to 0 in their match after they had a few wins in their bracket. That gave the Connecticut ruggers some confidence before they faced the URI "A" team in the finals. Their confidence didn't last long. They scored first and held a quick 6 to 0 lead but then Rhody reeled off 42 straight points and punctuated the win with a lopsided score of 42 to 6. Central Connecticut left the post party award ceremonies before the URI team arrived. Craig and I both had three tries in this final match and Jay T, "Tats", and Reed each had one score.

Some of the key "A" players on our sevens teams that changed over the years due to graduation, etc. consisted of myself, Rob, Barry R, Harry, Reed, Craig, Kent, Paul T, Ricky West, Joe "Rox" Rock, the Tagliardi brothers, Paul Seddon, Eddie "Steak" House, Jake, Barry "Soup" Sales, John "Nags" Nagel, "Tats", Ethan, and Lenny T.

I like the gloomy background of this New York Sevens 1979 final match photo below. We demolished Central Connecticut College. Both team's jerseys were a similar blue color and the referees that day made URI wear one of the other college's jerseys. So in this final match, we all wore red. I totally forgot about this scenario but I do vaguely remember that I was upset because I couldn't cut the sleeves off. In this photo, I have the ball and Reed is racing up the pitch with me. I didn't like to pass much. (Photo by G. Desisto)

Below are three pages of the 1979 New York Sevens Rugby Tournament's program preview. We won again as mentioned above – three in a row.

NEW YORK RUGBY FOOTBALL CLUB, INC.

AND

MANUFACTURERS HANOVER TRUST COMPANY

22nd Annual Sevens Tournament

SATURDAY, NOVEMBER 24, 1979, RANDALL'S ISLAND, NEW YORK CITY.

This page of the preview explains rugby sevens' techniques and strategy. I'm sure this helped many teams before each match.

NEW YORK
RUGBY FOOTBALL CLUB

RUGBY SEVEN

The Seven Techniques of Sevens

1. GAIN AND RETAIN POSSESSION: Possession is 99.9 per cent of the game. By possession is meant quality possession; once won, it must be retained, by good, constant support work and good handling. You cannot win without it and the opposition cannot score without it.
2. AREA DISCIPLINE: The field should be divided into seven areas running parallel with the touchline. A player should be placed in each area. Positional discipline should be maintained in both attack and defense.
3. CONTROL TEMPO: The tempo of the game should be controlled by retaining possession, good support and making the ball do the work.
4. RUN OFF THE BALL: The technique of the swivel line should be employed. Always try to have one man behind the man with the ball. This will ensure good support for the man in possession.
5. DEFENSIVE ALIGNMENT: The best method of defense is the straight-line defense with the cover being provided by a sweeper (scrum half) lying 9m. (10 yd.) back and in line with the ball. He is supported by the blindside winger. Marking should be man for man with area discipline observed.
6. NEVER BE ISOLATED: Always run towards support. No player should ever become isolated.
7. PRESSURE: Seven is a pressure game: when you have possession of the ball aim to gush the initiative and challenge the opposition, always being careful to keep the ball away from pressure; when the opposition have possession attempt to pressure them into making errors which forces a breakdown.

ABOVE ALL ELSE, SEVENS IS A THINKING GAME DEMANDING CONCENTRATION AND EFFORT, PARTICULARLY WHEN YOU ARE NOT IN POSSESSION OF THE BALL. RUNNING OFF THE BALL IS VITAL. SEVENS IS A GAME IN WHICH EVERYBODY IS IN THE GAME ALL THE TIME.

Rugby sevens strategy

PATTERN OF PLAY

1. Primary possession is vital. Once the ball has been won, take the initiative from the set piece and attack with the ball. Run the game at the opposition to challenge and pressure them.
2. Never put yourself into a situation where you feel pressured by the opposition. Always move the ball away into the open space before attempting to run forward to challenge the opposition. Whenever you are pressured pass the ball to an unmarked colleague who is free from danger.

ATTACKING TACTICS

3. When challenged by the opposition, try to turn your back and pass the ball to a supporting player who should (if the swivel line is in operation) be standing behind you. If the ball is stuck in a maul or ruck, the nearest player to the breakdown should go in to win the ball, be he a three quarter or forward.
3. After a pick-up following a ruck or a maul, the player picking up the ball should pass to a colleague. The rhythm, 'pass, pass, run', should be developed.

DEFENSIVE STRATEGY

1. Form the straight defense line as soon as possible. Then, maintaining the straight line, try to move up on your ponents slowly but surely trying to pressure them and force them to move backwards.

The "79" program also showed many of the college and men's clubs that competed that year. It was also the 50th anniversary of the sponsor – New York RFC, est. 1929.

SYRACUSE UNIVERSITY R.F.C.
WINGED FOOT R.F.C.
M.I.T. WOMEN'S R.F.C.
SYRACUSE UNIV. WOMEN'S R.F.C.
U. OF TENNESSEE R.F.C.
ITHACA OLD BOYS R.F.C.
CORTLAND ALL RED R.F.C.
MONTCLAIR R.F.C.
OLD GOLD R.F.C.
CENTRAL CONN. STATE COLLEGE R.F.C.
BOSTON COLLEGE R.F.C.
BOWDOIN COLLEGE R.F.C.
MANHATTAN R.F.C.
OLD GREEN R.F.C.
RICHMOND VA. R.F.C.
WASHINGTON R.F.C.
SETON HALL R.F.C.
BEAVER VALLEY R.F.C.
CONNECTICUT CLAMS R.F.C.
FROSTBURG R.F.C.
DREW UNIVERSITY R.F.C.
RUTGERS R.F.C.
CONNECTICUT YANKEES R.F.C.
MONTCLAIR WOMEN'S R.F.C.
S.U.N.Y. BUFFALO R.F.C.
CORTLAND STATE WOMEN'S R.F.C.
BERLIN STROLLERS R.F.C.
S.U.N.Y. BROCKPORT R.F.C.
UNIVERSITY OF RHODE ISLAND R.F.C.
WEST HARTFORD R.F.C.
NORWICH R.F.C.
F.D.U. ALUMNI R.F.C.
ROCKAWAY R.F.C.
NEW YORK R.F.C.
OLD BLUE R.F.C.
WESTCHESTER R.F.C.
OLD MAROON R.F.C.
BINGHAMPTON R.F.C.
MONTREAL WOMEN'S R.F.C.
BEAN TOWN WOMEN'S R.F.C.
BALTIMORE R.F.C.
MONTAUK R.F.C.
HUNTER R.F.C.
COLUMBIA R.F.C.
ESSEX R.F.C.
MONMOUTH R.F.C.
LONG ISLAND R.F.C.
PHILADELPHIA R.F.C.

WELCOME

Below is a New York Times article (in two separate pieces) that was written after one of those New York Sevens tournaments that we won. The scores and results didn't make it to the newspaper until the next day – so much for technology back then but the finals were always late due to the number of teams entered.

THE NEW YORK TIMES, SUNDAY, NOVEMBER 26,

A Day for Rugby 'Ruffians'

Beantown rugby players closing in on ball carrier from White Plains.

By MICHAEL STRAUSS

"This is a game for ruffians played by gentlemen, as opposed to soccer, which is a game for gentlemen played by ruffians," said Ed Lebow, the vice president of the host New York Rugby Club, yesterday, as more than 400 men and women gathered for their annual booting, tackling and passing jamboree on Randalls Island.

Lebow, a 44-year-old Manhattan travel agent who became a devotee of the game 17 years ago, emphasized that the "ruffians," phrase was not his own.

"It's a saying that is almost as old as the sport itself," said Lebow. "The game originated at England's Rugby School, where gentlemen sent their youngsters to be properly schooled. But even gentlemen's children like rough games, and rugby became part of the curriculum."

A Bit Too Windy

Yesterday's weather was not ideal for rugby. Players, representing 28 clubs and 16 colleges appeared on the windswept island wearing ski parkas, leather warmup pants, gloves and ear muffs. While playing, however, they stripped to thin shorts and cotton jerseys.

"This day would have been ideal except for the wind," said Lebow. "Our game calls for so much action that a player warms up almost immediately." But having to wait around during the long program that began at 8 A.M. and continued until almost dusk kept teeth chattering.

The turnout of enthusiasts each year for the annual tournament on Randalls Island is so big that six pitches (fields) have to be used to complete the activity. In all, 126 games — each lasting 15 minutes — were played yesterday.

"This is a day on which we make adjustments," said Lebow, "otherwise it might take us until Christmas to complete a program this size."

Ordinarily a rugby team is made up of 15 players. They participate in two halves of 40 minutes each. But to keep everyone happy and busy on a day like this, periods and size of teams were cut. Seven players were on each team.

Participants from Afar

Yesterday's turnout included men and women from such campuses as

McGill University in Montreal, Syracuse, Cortland State, Norwich University and Rhode Island. Club players came from as far away as Chicago. There were even participants who had learned the game in New Zealand and Samoa.

"When we started from Montreal last Friday, there were six inches of snow on the ground, and it was snowing," said Kim Scholefield, the McGill squad's scrum half. "This whole Indian summer for us, and even the drive down from Canada was hairy. The interstate highway through the Adirondacks was only a one-lane deal."

Despite the seven-man teams, yesterday's games followed regular rugby rules in which taking the ball, running with it, dribbling it with the feet and passing it with the hands, were all part of the pattern. The pitches were of regulation size — approximately 110 yards long and 75 yards wide.

CHAPTER 7

Some of the characters

"Success in golf depends less on strength of body than upon strength of mind and character."

Arnold Palmer – One of the great American professional golfers and legends.

I can't detail each and every URI teammate that I played with or enjoyed their friendship but there are a few Rhody Ruggers that I have to mention before I go any further in this book. These are just a few members of the Rhode Island Rugby Club that were on many of the teams that helped make this athletic club special.

Most of the players mentioned were the "A" team ruggers because that was our varsity team and that was the team that I spent most of my time with. I knew many of the other players who were on the "B" team as well, but this was the team I went to battle with on every match Saturday and together we went after it each rugby weekend during the school year seasons.

Rox was one of the few larger pack players who also competed on our sevens teams. He played wing forward in fifteens and was part of the scrum in my later years that could compete with the better men's teams in New England. He was another good high school athlete out of Barrington, Rhode Island who matched well with Mick Kenyon, another pack player on and off the rugby field.

They were both notorious for partying quite late at other campus or off campus parties after our rugby parties had ended. Sometimes, we had early morning home matches and both Rox and Mick had some trouble waking up and playing in those early matches. I wondered why in some of our matches we scored more of our tries in the second half.

When most of the other teams we played were slowing down after a very physical and bruising first half, we seemed to be getting stronger and faster, especially the forwards.

Mick played basketball at East Greenwich High School in Rhode Island and dabbled in other sports before he came to URI. His nickname was "Sasquatch" and he had quite the reputation with the college coeds. I'm not sure how he discovered the Rhody Ruggers but we were sure glad to have him, especially for lineouts.

Mick is in the middle of a lineout in the photo below. He didn't lose too many of these throw-ins. (Photo by G. Desisto)

The Tagliardi brothers were an integral part of the URI Rugby Team in my later rugby years and they were both captains of the team at different times. Mike's first position in rugby was at outside center but after playing many matches at this position and even though he was a tough runner, some of the team selection officers thought he would be better suited as a scrum-half.

A year or so later during a volatile team selection process that led to some dissension on the team (Some players quit the team.), he was voted to play this new position on the "A" team. This is where he discovered his better suited skills in rugby and he became a very good scrum-half due to his tenacity and quickness. Of course, Mike had to fill the vacant shoes of our previous scrum-half – "Dirty Harry."

Dirty Harry's real name was Harry Westler and as his name suggests he was one of the toughest players on our team. Playing "dirty" in rugby doesn't mean what it means in other sports. Rugby is a "dirty" game to begin with. There is only one referee during a rugby match. There are two other officials called line or touch judges. They help call extra point and penalty goal kicks, out of play sideline ball locations, throw-ins, and other calls that the main referee can't see well or needs assistance with due to his positioning on the pitch.

But the one referee's ruling on the rugby field is the final ruling (He is also called "god".) with little or no negotiation with these touch judges who work the sidelines. This leads to some bad and missed calls and the players take advantage of this. This was called gamesmanship, not playing dirty.

Rugby mauls and rucks that occur frequently during a match with large piles of ruggers on top of each other sometimes ended up with punches, kicks, scratching, and even some biting during these matches. Harry was a great scrum-half who made sure the backs received the ball quickly so we could move down the pitch and away from the pack but his violent tackling skills were legendary and not necessarily dirty. He could throw an elbow or forearm when needed but when we played back then, you would only receive a warning if a tackle was considered excessive or illegal and were never thrown out of a match.

There was a match against a men's club from New York that actually asked one of our captains if we could take Harry out of the match because he hurt a few of their players but the referee had no reason to eject him from the match; they were all clean tackles.

This photo shows Harry preparing for a lineout. Reed is the weak side wing in the background and Steve "Bales" Bailey one of our props is on Harry's right. (Photo by G. Desisto)

Harry received many warnings and that's where his nickname came from. I received a few warnings myself over the years – not because of a vicious tackle, that I did have my share of, but because I liked to tackle some of my opponents high around the head or neck. This was called "head hunting" and I did this frequently when playing against taller, stronger ruggers. It might not have been legal but it just seemed the natural place to hit tall opponents and most of them hated getting hit in the head so I did it to try to intimidate the opposing team members – more gamesmanship.

Jay, Mike's younger brother also played outside center and we worked well together. He was very fast but also had great ball fakes and could cut back well into the middle of the rugby field at any time. This allowed him options to pass to me or the other winger or fake the pass and keep the ball himself and take it to the house for a try. "Swivel hips" was one of his nicknames. The other thing I remember about Jay was that he had no lack of confidence when he first began playing this new game he had never played before and he was one of the biggest ball busters on the team. "JTags" is what we called him.

He continued playing for a local city club when he graduated from URI and also continued competing in seven-a-side matches with the URI Old Boys, the URI alumni sevens team who competed in various sevens tournaments – at both the regional and national levels.

The photo below shows JTags with a nice open field tackle against one of our opponents in a 1980 spring match. He was a solid defensive player as well as a great offensive threat. (Photo by Yearbook staff)

The two brothers were talented high school athletes who played various sports for their New Jersey Cedar Grove hometown high school. Mike played football and wrestled and JTags played basketball and baseball.

In the next photo - JTags with the ball is seen making one of his patented "cuts" while Craig and Paul T, next to him on both sides, follow him past a few opponents. His hips were moving well. (Photo by G. Desisto)

Eddie "Steak" House lived in the Sigma Chi fraternity next door to my fraternity. We became good friends through rugby and started hanging out socially before he graduated and entered the Peace Corps. We exchanged letters for a few more of my rugby seasons while he worked in Africa. He played wing forward and number eight in the pack and played with URI at the beginning of the team's early growth and success. His hair was totally grey and some of the girls thought he looked like Paul Newman, or so Steak told me.

John "Nags" Nagel was a forward who graduated in 1977 with my class and he played second row, wing forward, and prop – a very versatile rugger. He grew up in New York and was also a large part of our team's early success. After he graduated from URI, he played for another ten or twelve years with some of the local men's clubs in Connecticut. He still loves to talk "rugby". A few years ago, he tried to coordinate a competitive "URI Old Boys" fifteens team, a very old "Old Boys" team. I'm not sure if he was serious or not – but it never happened. We all knew better.

Peter Bennett was one of the original "seventies" ruggers who started playing at URI with Lenny Dawson and Cole Smith; all tough scrum players who were heavily involved with the club prior to me joining the team and they helped organize and recruit numerous players. He played prop and graduated before me but he didn't get to see how far the team progressed in our later years. He was also a punishing tackler.

Ray Gallucci was a Westerly police officer who dabbled in boxing when he was younger and competed in a few "Golden Glove" tournaments. He was a total animal on the pitch playing in the scrum and he would eat lit cigarettes at the parties. Off the field, he was a great guy and very calm.

Steve Bailey and Tim Meek both played prop, both had blonde hair, both were in fraternities, both had steady girl friends when they played and were nicknamed the "bookends". During their playing days, they were quite large and helped the pack with a strong push. After their rugby careers ended, they lost much of their extra weight by running and working out and they both completely changed their physical appearance. Steve joined the Navy after graduation and achieved a very high rank in this branch of the service. Tim attained a business degree and joined the corporate world after he graduated.

Jake Knowles was a large part of our very successful sevens teams that did well at the various sevens tournaments we participated in over the years. He was tall, played inside center, possessed a great stiff arm when running with the ball, and shared some of the extra point and penalty kicking duties. He was another very good high school athlete who discovered the URI Rugby Club and he played football and basketball prior to college.

Barry "Soup" Sales took over the very important fly-half position for our team when Rob left. Soup played many sports in high school and was the most intelligent rugby player on any of the URI teams I played with. He majored in Zoology and became a research scientist in the Oceanography department at one of the local state colleges and visits Antarctica a few times per year on special projects related to his work. Soup also continued playing rugby for many years; he played for the Providence RFC and was part of the URI Old Boys very good sevens teams. After a URI match, he would try to duck out of the party early or not even attend the party because he had to study. That never worked – we always made sure we found him and sometimes physically carried him to the party and forced him to have at least a few beers or pints with the team.

Soup, in this photo, looks like he is intending to punt the ball over the Providence RFC player – Bob Cagney who played both football and rugby at URI before he graduated and moved back to his hometown of Barrington. "Cags" later became a high school teacher and football coach.
(Photo by G. Desisto)

Nick Weston or "Wes" was one of the numerous Rhody Ruggers who lived in a fraternity at URI – Phi Gamma Delta. Our team consisted of many players who joined various fraternities when I played. Wes played prop and wing forward and was one of the reasons that the pack played so well in the late seventies. He was also a great singer at the parties and always played the "Muffin Man" game. Paul Thayer was the backup Muffin Man and he was also very good in this event.

Wes actually had a very nice voice and was a large part of his fraternity's many "Greek Sing Contest" wins during "Greek Week" at URI. Greek Week consisted of a week at the end of each school year when all the fraternities and sororities were pitted against each other and competed in various games and activities.

At the end of the week, an overall champion was crowned for each fraternity and sorority based on total points awarded for each contest. Wes' fraternity approached these games very seriously and won many of these Greek Week championships.

My fraternity, Sigma Nu finished in last place most of the years we participated in the "Greek Sing" event held in the old "Keaney" gymnasium before the "Ryan Center" was built. Gary Point who majored in Education and became a high school music teacher after college was our not so proud chorus leader.

One year, I volunteered to be in the famous "Chariot Race" held in the football stadium. We won that year from what I remember during this very busy week with school and so many rugby and Greek events going on with two Rhody Ruggers – Vinnie Patrone and I, Paul Crowley, our frat's intramural football quarterback, and Mike Lauro – a talented and strong weight thrower on the URI Track team. Mike also competed in the beer keg throw during this fun week and did well in this event. The driver of the chariot that day was Joe Pothier and he had the most dangerous job steering the makeshift chariot. Part of this event consisted of building the chariot and making sure it crossed the finish line with the driver still intact or the team was disqualified.

In the photo below from left to right, the chariot relay team consisted of me, Paul, Mike, and Vinnie. This event was held in the football stadium and was quite popular even in the rain. I love the "short"' shorts we wore back then. Funny, rugby hasn't changed this style, shorts are still short unlike basketball or soccer shorts – maybe less to grab on to for the defensive players. (Photo by a Sigma Nu brother)

After one of the New England Rugby Union open tournaments, Wes bought over thirty colorful rugby bumper stickers with various humorous or inappropriate rugby sayings on them from one of the vendors who attended these matches. He then proceeded to cover his latest girlfriend's car's rear bumper and trunk with all of them. The car was fairly new and they had been dating for only a week or so.

Below is a photo of one of the rugby bumper stickers that I saved for my scrap book that I bought at one of those New England tournaments. I had one just like this on my Ford Pinto but when I landed a teaching job, I replaced it with a nicer slogan – "RUGBY BECAUSE."

Kevin Horton, George McKay, and Ricky were three of the hookers who played well in the Rhode Island scrum during the years when URI matured as a rugby team. They each had their own style but all three were about the same height and weight and excelled at controlling the ball with their feet. Hooker has to be one of the toughest forward positions in the scrum because it all starts with a big "push" and the hooker is the main point of contact with the opposing hooker and the other scrum members. Hooker injuries were very common in rugby matches.

SCRAMBLE: Members of the URI Rugby club jockey for position in last weekend's contest against the Charles River club. The Rams won 54-0 and in the last two games have outscored their opponents 100-3.

Ricky in the photo below working on his "hooker" skills with props – Wes and Howie Stewart during a practice. (Photo by Five Cent Cigar)

Terry Timmons, a URI professor is in the photo below and is ready to release the ball at a practice to Mike T or myself and Ray Ankles and Jake are following the line. (Photo by Yearbook staff)

The color photo below shows those newer URI jerseys that we wore in my later years. At that point, we did try to dress like an official rugby team. I started wearing dark blue shorts to match the shirt but it looks like my socks have green stripes. Don "Boomer" Remy played outside center that day and Paul T in the background was our full-back. Notice my sleeves were cutoff and tape was only on one thumb and wrist. (Photo by L. O'Neil)

CHAPTER 8

A few of our best matches

"The only important statistic is the final score."

Bill Russell – Retired Hall of Fame American professional basketball player who won eleven NBA championships with the Boston Celtics in his thirteen-year career.

Many of us played rugby for the University of Rhode Island Rugby Club for more than a few years due to various reasons such as continuing with our education in a master's program, not graduating in four years, working in the area, or living in the area close to the beach communities outside of Kingston in the surrounding small towns because it was a great place to live. We hung out after matches and practices and enjoyed each other's friendship and this showed on the rugby field.

I believe part of our success as a team was due to the fact that many of us bonded well together when we were first introduced to this foreign game even though we all came from different sports backgrounds. There was no official coach and we all started at the same level – freshman rugby players. As we practiced more and competed in more matches, we evolved and the players who had more experience taught the next set of novice rugby players and then those players taught the next set and so on and so forth.

The post parties that we all attended after each match also made our club a closer, tight group of players which does not happen in other sports. These traditional parties were part of the rugby experience. So even though the URI Rugby Club consisted of various fraternity and dorm students, off campus housing students, undergraduates, graduate students, and some alumni – all from many different backgrounds and states – we all came together on the pitch. As I noted previously, we had two or three full teams when the club was strong so everybody played but it was up to the individual to prove to himself and the club what team he would represent on match day Saturdays.

This happened with the competition during each practice and match throughout the season so there should have been no blame or argument when the selectors picked each team on Friday. If you played well in practice or a match and stood out in your respective position, then you would be rewarded with a spot on the "A" or "B" team side on Saturday. I'm sure there were some tough decisions each selection day but this club was not a dictatorship with one or two "coaches" – we were all coaches in some way.

There were some leaders of course and some teammates who were more vocal concerning issues and disagreements but for the most part, we were one family and it showed on the pitch. I never participated in the selection committees and I never held a club office; I just played the "game".

URI ruggers capture Harvard tourney title

Special to the Journal-Bulletin
CAMBRIDGE, Mass. — The University of Rhode Island's rugby team swept through six matches and won the annual Harvard Business School Tournament championship yesterday.

The Rams beat Hartford, Conn., 10-3, in the championship

Page 10 November 15, 1978 The Good 5¢ Cigar

URI rugby ends with 'best game' of season

Ruggers defy weather, rip White Plains, 34-6

rolled past the baffled White Plains defense

by Sherri O'Connor
Cigar Sports Staff

Ram 'A' team ruggers take 'biggest' tourney

by Peter Boggs
Cigar Sports Staff

handled Iona 18-6, and skipped by Syracuse 14-10 in sudden death overtime. This

so good since we'd never heard of them before, but they had already beaten Princeton and Tennessee.

—— Dominates New England college scene ——

URI rugby club hits the big-time

Spring 1978 – URI vs. White Plains RFC (fifteen-a-side)

In 1978, Rob scheduled a match against a very good men's team from White Plains, New York, located close to where he grew up and a team that he would later play with after he completed his master's degree program at URI. It was a home match so this would benefit us due to the wider rugby field that we sometimes prepared that I never knew about until my career was over. This was also called gamesmanship and I did see this same type of strategy occur when other teams played against us and they set up their fields with a very short sideline to offset our team's running skills and speed.

We played the first half in a heavy rain that day and both teams were affected by this bad weather. It made ball handling, passing, and running much more difficult and each player seemed to possess the same speed on the slick, grass rugby pitch. It was only 10 to 0 in our favor after the first half. We had two scores and one conversion by Kent Chase who played wing forward and number eight in the scrum but also kicked for us from time to time. He played soccer in high school and had a very strong leg and kicked with great accuracy.

This bad weather really helped the New York club and their backs played our backs very flat and matched each of us very well. In the second half, the rain subsided and we exploded for five tries. The drier pitch helped our backs' running game and the pack did well against this veteran men's club to supply us with the ball often.

Reed and I both scored twice in that match. Reed was one of the many walk-ons for the Rhode Island football team when colleges carried a freshman junior varsity team. I think he played wide receiver for that team but in rugby, he played outside center and wing. He was tall and fast and was a great asset to our sevens teams because he could play in the scrum but then when the pack broke up, he was another speedy back. He continued playing rugby with the Providence RFC and the URI Old Boys sevens team for many years after graduating from URI.

Reed's girlfriend at the time – Gail, whom he later married, was also the unofficial team photographer. She took many photos of the team over the years and helped some of us compile scrap books of our rowdy, rugby days.

The other scorers that day were JTags and Ricky, our hooker during that spring. It was nice to see the forwards get a score in that match because they played so well against the veteran White Plains pack.

Lenny T and Mike Votta both had great games for our pack in this match as well. They were gaining more experience with the "A" team after they had recently moved up from the "B" team. The other two standouts that helped supply a strong push and controlled many lineout possessions when the ball was thrown in from out of bounds possessions were the veteran duo of Mick and Rox. Mick stood tall at six foot six and was a great leaper on lineouts and Rox at six feet two with a wider build could also jump.

Lenny T below is racing up the pitch after picking up a loose ball out of a scrum. This shows why he also played for the sevens teams, he ran with the backs. Towards the end of his career, Lenny wore a "skull cap" to protect his ears.

BREAKING OUT: URI's Len Thibodeau clears the ball after a scrum. The Ruggers recently won the New York Sevens Tournament and will play in the national Sevens tournament to be held in Hartford next June. (Cigar photo by Scott Ramsay)

One of the novice ruggers who played for White Plains that day later became a United States National rugby player on the Eagles Select Side – Gary Lambert. The National Rugby Team was nicknamed "The Eagles". He played flanker in the pack for the Eagles in 1981. This was one of the first men's club matches he had played in and even then – you knew he was something special.

The final score on that dreary day was 34 to 6. Rob knew many of the players and the party after was very tame. I think White Plains was pretty subdued due to losing to a small college team even though they had heard we had a very competitive team. They also had a long car ride home after a bitter defeat so they were not up for late night partying. Rugby teams in the seventies and eighties didn't seem to travel in buses or vans – I know we never did. We always drove our own cars and trucks and back then – the term "designated driver" didn't exist. Lucky for us, we did have some serious ruggers on our team and they were responsible chauffeurs. None of us had a serious accident during my rugby traveling days but there were a few auto mishaps. Drinking and driving definitely does not mix!

Rob ended up playing for the White Plains RFC for over fifteen years after leaving the University of Rhode Island with his Physical Education Master's degree. He taught for a few years somewhere in his home state but at some point, he left teaching and opened up a small bar and restaurant. This was very convenient for rugby postgame parties of course.

Fall 1978 – URI vs. Charles River RFC (fifteen-a-side)

In the fall of 1978, we played the Charles River Rugby Football Club on their home rugby field in Boston. It was difficult to beat any team on their own turf. Charles River had beaten the Old Gold RFC earlier in the season and Old Gold trounced us the week before with a score of 15-0. We couldn't have played any worse and could not put the ball in the goal area. I think this is the match that I actually tripped on my own spike laces when they got loose and I had a shot at a breakaway score. (I used to wear very long laces in my spikes.) It was just one of those days.

The sign of a good rugby team is how they respond after a loss and we did respond.

We kept the pressure on Charles River in the first half but just like the previous week – the opponent's defense held up and we couldn't score. At the end of the half, we were ahead with a slight lead of 6-0. In the second half, the Rhody Ruggers turned up the intensity and both the backs and the forwards played much better. After the match, Rob our captain told the team that the second half was the best half we had played all year and he confirmed what all of us thought – we played as one unit. We also had some ruggers playing with injuries – Rob hadn't played in four weeks due to a bad bone bruise in his arm and JTags was playing with a broken finger. It didn't matter.

JTags scored two tries, I scored one try, and Rob scored another on one of his usual fakes to the inside center and then a quick dash right up the middle of the pitch when we were within striking distance of Charles River's goal area. Paul T handled the kicking that day and had two conversion kicks and a penalty kick and the pack dominated the entire second half. Tats had a great game for the forwards. The final score was Rhody – 23, Charles River – 0.

The "B" team won a tight match also in a defensive battle with a score of 8-3. Will Sinton and Kyle Madigan had the two tries. It was the last match of the season and the "A" team ended that fall with an 8 and 1 record including five shutouts. We then went on to win the New York Sevens Tournament on Thanksgiving weekend.

Spring 1979 – URI vs. Providence RFC (fifteen-a-side)

For years, the Providence RFC men's club only allowed their "B" team to play against the Rhody Ruggers "A" team. After a few Providence "B" team defeats and prompting by Rob and the other URI match selection committee members, Providence eventually agreed to play their "A" team against our "A" team on their home field behind Hope High School in Providence in 1979.

That year, we were on a roll and undefeated in the spring season with a 7 and 0 record. Providence was also having a good year. Providence was the second best men's team in New England in fifteens during that spring season and they thought they were well prepared for us. Bob Hoder knew us quite well and he figured the Providence pack could control the match so our backs wouldn't get many chances to score. He was wrong.

The strength of the forwards that day especially – Mick and Rox and our two props that we called the "bookends" helped our pack win many scrum downs and various rucks and mauls. That led to Rob and JTags creating havoc with their elusive cutbacks and creative passing that led to a total blowout.

Providence scored first with George Smith, a pack player getting the first try and Warren Boothman or "Turkey" as they called him, kicked the easy conversion. Warren now coaches at URI with some other veteran Providence ruggers. This current URI team plays in a legitimate college division and each year they contend for a championship in this Northeast league. The days of mixing men's teams with colleges and university teams are over.

We also seemed to wear down the Providence veteran club team with our usual mixture of short and long runs. Two of their players may have actually left the match with pulled hamstrings that day (I am not sure.) due to the speed that we flashed during that match. That also meant Providence had played the final few minutes of the match with only 13 ruggers and a comeback from Providence was nowhere in sight. As I said in one of the previous chapters, substitutions even for injuries didn't exist when I played.

We ended up scoring 22 points in the second half. JTags scored three times, twice with a nice fake outside pass to me and then a nice cutback all the way to the goal line area. I had two long outside tries set up by JTags when he did deliver the ball to me and Rob had the final score. All the conversion kicks which were in the middle of the goal area were easily kicked by Kent. In rugby, the conversion kick is located where the rugby ball is downed on a try. So, if you score in the corner of the end line, you must kick from that location of the pitch. Corner tries make the conversion kick much more difficult.

John Hoder closed out the Providence scoring with a try and we won the match with a final score of 30 to 10. Bob Hoder also played in this big match win for Rhody.

Bobby Cagney from Barrington, Rhode Island, another ex-football player at URI who played one season with our team in the spring was also on this Providence RFC team that day. Even though "Cags" had less than two years' experience under his belt playing rugby, he played like a veteran rugger already. He was a superb athlete in high school competing in various sports and was one of the most highly touted University of Rhode Island freshman football recruits in 1973 – he played linebacker for four years on this team. I made sure I didn't get close to him when I was running with the ball.

Providence was not happy with the final score of the match because it wasn't even close. But most of them knew there would be better days ahead for their team when some of these same players that had just kicked their butts would graduate and return to Providence to play with them. This win also proved that the young Rhody Ruggers had a good pack as well as a good set of backs and we could compete with many of the men's clubs in New England.

The photo below shows the "Pack" running hard up the pitch after a loose ball ended up in the hands of one of these great forwards – Mick and Rox are behind the passer. JTags is trailing this play, back left. (Photo by G. Desisto)

Spring 1979 – URI vs. the touring 'Stars' from France (fifteen-a-side)

It was a strange time to play a home rugby match but at 3 pm on a Monday afternoon, a rugby team that consisted of a select side from three Veterinarian schools in France took the rugby field and began their warm-ups. One of the ruggers on this team had a friend or a relative that lived in the Phi Mu Delta fraternity house on campus and they had stayed there the previous night. They were scheduled to play a few American teams during their road trip including one of the New York men's rugby select teams but today they were going to play against the University of Rhode Island Rugby Football Club.

I remember watching them warm up. They were quiet and very professional with their drills and warm-up routines that I had never seen before. They also had some very large athletes and I thought we might have over scheduled by committing to this team that looked very good as we were going through our usual helter-skelter warm-up routines that consisted of groups and individuals doing their own thing.

After about twenty minutes, the French team then formed a huddle and their coach – Vic Picolo spoke to his team for another ten minutes. We didn't even have a coach.

After that session, there were a few short ceremonies that included photographs of some of the URI players taken by the French team to help them remember the teams they played and the cities they visited. There was also an exchange of a few small gifts between the players of each team; I still have the French medal that we received that day. I guess that was all planned but I knew nothing about any of that and was getting quite itchy, waiting for the initial kickoff. I just wanted to play.

The visitors wasted no time scoring. Yves Dubois blocked one of our players' kicks at our own 15-meter line and another French player pounced on the loose ball in our goal area to score the first try of the match with only six minutes into the match. A few minutes later, Michael Panisse for France connected on a penalty kick 30 meters out and the French team was now leading URI – 7 to 0. We did not look good!

After these two quick scores, we settled down and Mick gave a great pass to Barry R on the visitor's 30-meter line and he outran two or three of their "all-stars" for a try in the corner. The score remained 7 to 4 until the second half when Jake blocked one of their kicks and I picked up the bouncing ball cleanly in their goal area for an easy try – "garbage man" time. Rob made the conversion kick and we were now up 10 to 7. After that goal, we took over and applied our pressure defense combined with our usual speed in the pack and in the backfield and we reeled off the next sixteen straight points.

The match ended with Rhody defeating this "Stars" team with the final score: 26 to 7. After the match, Coach Picolo discussed the outcome using a translator.

"The Americans played very nice rugby. They were the masters of playing the game today. They wanted to win and they did."

I don't remember the party that early Monday evening but I do remember the French team was very gracious with the loss and seemed like a nice group of gentlemen ruggers. None of them were out of control during the party and the party didn't last very long because they had to leave early the next day to travel and prepare for the next American team they had scheduled.

Spring 1979 – URI vs. Hartford RFC (Harvard Sevens tournament finals)

This was before the Buffalo Bills played in four straight Super Bowls and lost each one. Many considered this NFL football team a "bad" team but no other team made it to the Super Bowl for four straight years. That feat itself tagged the Bills as one of the great teams in the history of the NFL and it consisted of many All-Stars and Hall of Fame members including Jim Kelly, the quarterback for all of those years and Thurman Thomas, the great running back.

The University of Rhode Island RFC was the Buffalo Bills of rugby sevens teams back in 1979. This was our fourth straight Harvard (HBS) Sevens finals and we lost the previous three. We were matched against a team that had already won at least one Harvard Sevens Tournament and was also a very accomplished fifteens team. Barry Richards had moved to Hartford and he was now playing against us. Tommy Vinick played center that day for this very good men's team and years later he played for the United States National Rugby "Eagles" team in 1987.

I don't remember much of the match other than it was a low scoring, defensive chess match. I scored a cheap, short try in the corner of the left side of the pitch after we moved the ball up close to their goal. Reed cemented the victory when he ran back a kickoff right up the middle of the pitch after a Hartford penalty goal kick. I don't think any opposing player touched him on that nifty run. The final score was 10 to 3 and we finally won this elusive tournament. I felt bad for Barry but one of us had to win that day and snap the three year losing streak.

The teams we beat that day and the final scores of the matches were:

Mystic River 16 – 0

Brown University 18 – 0

Coast Guard B 22 – 0

Beacon Hill 16 – 6

Washington Exiles 30 – 4

This special win or the 1978 New York Sevens Tournament win also qualified URI for the National Sevens Tournament later that summer in Hartford, Connecticut with other rugby football club sevens tournament champions.

The photo above shows Rob handing out the Harvard Sevens Champion mugs in 1979. I'm holding the team trophy as well – not sure who has that rugby collectible today but maybe we had to return it the next year. Paul T and Will are on my right and a few other ruggers are in the background wearing their Keaney Blue Rhody Rugby jackets. (Photo by D. Frye)

Below are two pages of the HBS Sevens Rugby Tournament's program preview that all the players and fans received each year. This one I saved – we finally won defeating the Hartford RFC after losing three previous straight finals. The second page explains the "sevens" game in simpler terms.

the 15th Annual HBS

Seven-A-Side Rugby

Tournament

Sunday, May 6 . 1979

9:30 am-6:30 pm
at Harvard Business School
Soldiers Field , Boston

THE SEVEN-A-SIDE GAME

This form of the game has been a traditional finale to the season in Britain and its popularity has crossed the Atlantic. It provides more thrills per minute, and open field running than most sports can offer. There are only two more players per side than on a basketball court, and they cover an area bigger than a football field. None of the laws are changed for this form of mini-rugby. Each team fields three forwards, two half-backs and two three-quarters. Although each game lasts only 14 minutes you won't see many players finishing a game without heaving chests and sweaty brows.

The good 'sevens' team has three essential elements. It has forwards who can win the ball in the lines-out and scrums (possession being nine-tenths of the law), a couple of experienced players who can slow the game down to conserve the team's energy, and one or two real speedsters who can exploit the wide open spaces down the sidelines. Today's tournament contains the best teams from all over New England. The one that emerges victorious will have exhibited a combination of brains, brawn, stamina and good fortune.

PARTICIPATING TEAMS

Old North Bridge	Tufts
Brown	Old Gold
Old Bone	Berlin Strollers
Hartford Wanderers	Scumbags
U-Mass Medical	Mystic River RFC
Mystic River	Portsmouth Seamen
University of Rhode Island	Holy Cross
U.S. Coast Guard Academy	Iona RFC
Massachusetts Institute of Technology	University of Massachusetts
Boston RFC	University of Connecticut
Washington Exiles	Beacon Hill RFC
Charles River RFC	Harvard Business School RFC
Portland Bushwackers	

CHAPTER 9

The pack

"You never win a game unless you beat the guy in front of you. The score on the board doesn't mean a thing."

Vince Lombardi – Hall of Fame American football player, coach, and executive of the Green Bay Packers NFL championship team.

In this book, I have concentrated on stories and events primarily associated with the backs that I played with during my rugby career. This is not to shortchange the forwards that were also a major part of our success during the seventies and early eighties. There are eight pack players that are also called forwards and these ruggers are usually larger, stronger, and heavier than the back players. These athletes that can be compared to the offensive and defensive front line of any American football team use their size and strength to capture or control the ball and move it towards the opposing team's goal line.

There were many great players in this specific subset of the URI Rugby Team but because I didn't venture much towards the middle of the pitch where these ruggers roamed, I can't tell you how they operated or who did what during these matches. I did my best to stay away from rucks and mauls, especially when the scrum was involved – it wasn't my type of game. They all were my friends and we partied together and of course hung out but their rugby skills and their match details I can't really comment on.

The other reason that I bonded more with the backs was that there was a greater number of rugby sevens tournaments than regular fifteen-a-side tournaments that URI competed in that could consist of playing five or six matches in one day if we made it to the finals. We became close in those sevens tournaments and sometimes stayed overnight at one of the rugger's homes who lived close to where the matches were located so we could be rested in the morning and well prepared for a long, physical day of rugby.

Only a few forwards were selected for these teams. Instead of using pack players in these three-men sevens' scrums, we participated in tournaments with our taller and larger backs (and a few wing forwards or number eights from the pack) and played them in the scrum. So after a ruck or a maul broke up – these "special" forwards became legitimate backs and that's what seemed to facilitate our successful long run at the New York and Harvard Sevens tournaments. Some of the Rhody forwards that also had sufficient speed and good ball handling skills to play with the "A" and "B" sevens teams over the years were:

Craig, Ethan, Nags, Steak, Ricky, Paul S, Rox, Lenny T, Wes, and Tats.

I do understand that the bottom line in any rugby match is – if the pack doesn't control the ball and push it back to the scrum-half, the backs aren't able to do what they do best. In rugby, you need a pack that can control and move the ball forward and also play tough defense against the other pack. The URI pack sometimes didn't seem to get enough of the credit for some of our big fifteen-a-side wins over the years because of our style of play but I know that didn't matter to any of them. They loved playing in the scrum and all the battles that they fought during those two forty-minute halves.

The pack positions in a scrum consists of the hooker who hooks the ball back to his own teammates – starting with the scrum-half, two props who hold up the hooker, two locks or second rows that lock in the prop, and two flankers who "bind" on the side of the scrum and help lock the major part of a scrum but can break away from the pack quickly to tackle the opposing ruggers or run with the ball. The last position is the number eight who completes the tight "bind" and helps create a better push for the entire pack. This player also breaks away from the scrum quickly and easily and can run with the ball like another back. The diagram below that I created shows the basic setup of a scrum when matched against another pack, head to head.

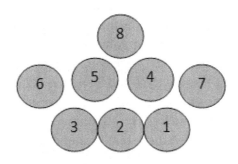

1 and 3 = prop, 2 = hooker, 6 and 7 = loose forward /flanker,
4 and 5 = lock /second row, 8 = number eight

The leader of the scrum and also one of the captains of the team when I first started playing rugby was a gentleman named Lenny Dawson, nicknamed "Cowboy". (This was not the great NFL quarterback.) Lenny grew up in Pennsylvania and played the prop position. He taught most of us about this foreign game but I'm not quite sure where he obtained this knowledge other than joining the URI Rugby Club after football didn't work out for him.

Over the years, there might have been a few URI ruggers that did have some previous experience playing rugby before joining our club. One of these ruggers from New York who actually played rugby in high school was Jim Hoges. He played inside center and had good quickness and great moves and ball fakes. Jim played on the "A" team right away when he joined our club.

Lenny was a strong, rugby forward with good size who helped supply our pack with a great push in the early years when he joined the team and he was very knowledgeable concerning the technical aspects of the game. He was also quite adept at controlling the parties after the matches with his entertaining rugby stories and various sing-a-longs that he would initiate with his singing partner – Doug (who was also very entertaining). I'd say he was the patriarch of the Rhody Rugby Club during my playing days even though the club was created many years previous in 1966. He currently teaches and coaches football at a private high school in Massachusetts.

The other leader and captain of those early mid-seventies teams who was another tough, hardnosed forward, and a fierce rugby competitor was Cole Smith. He played two years before I joined the club and suffered various wins and losses in those early seventies rugby years. He played wing forward or flanker and played football and wrestled in high school in Warwick, Rhode Island. He kept the team's spirits up during some of those early team losses and continued recruiting new athletes for the club.

The plan worked and in a few short years, the URI Rugby Football Club became an excellent college team that could compete with many of the men's teams in New England. Cole graduated a year before me and married Cindy – one of our famous "Rugby Managers". Rugby Managers were female students who helped the team with supplies such as water, first aid kits, sports tape, etc. and provided positive encouragement at practices and matches. The two original URI Rugby Managers were Donna Baron and Cindy Almonte. They were both freshmen when they started attending our rugby matches and they created this new club role on their own. They were such great kids.

Pictured below are Donna and Cindy from their senior graduation photos in the 1979 URI yearbook. They were best friends and they later became the team's best friends. Below their photos is a sample of their work – a homemade get well card for me when I cut my head in a match and missed the following match. (Stitches couldn't be removed for days.)

Other rugby managers that worked with the URI Rugby Club as well after Donna and Cindy graduated were: Janet Serdjenian (Janet married Craig after college.), Kendra Beaver, Joan Wolferseder, and Lynne Paynter. They were also a dedicated support team.

The left photo below shows Lenny D wearing a headband and controlling the ball after a short throw-in on a lineout. Ray G and Will control the ball in a maul in the right photo. (Photos by Yearbook staff)

Dillon Flynn, Caleb Collins, and most of the URI pack are trying to push one of our ball carriers into the goal area for a try in the photo below.
(Photo by Yearbook staff)

In the photo below, Rox goes high for a lineout. (Photo by Five Cent Cigar)Peter B in the right photo, a speedy forward is chasing down Andy Bullock during a practice scrimmage against ourselves and George, Ray A, and Mark Mattson are following the play. (Photo by Yearbook staff)

Below Ricky is away from his usual hooker position and controlling the ball in a maul. (Photo by G. Desisto)

Below, Cole, Nags, and Steak follow Cam Langer on a nice run up the middle of the rugby field where the forwards roam. (Photo by Yearbook staff) The bottom photo shows that the forwards are ready for the throw-in but both teams look a little tired – it must be close to the end of the second half. (Photo by L. O'Neil)

In a match with the Providence RFC below, both packs are fighting hard for possession of the ball and one of our ruggers is reaching for it when it's available for anybody. This shows what a scrum is really like with hands, feet, and bodies intertwined in the chaos that goes on in front of the backs.
(Photo by G. Desisto)

This photo highlights the Rhody forwards intensity in a lineout. Pictured back to front are Lenny T, Bales, Craig, Ray, Mike V, James Gains, and Wes. (Photo by G. Desisto)

Above in this photo is the beginning of a scrum down – Wes, James, Ricky, and Craig show the right side of our forwards that day. Backs in the background standing are Dave Glory (farthest back left side in the photo), Will, and Dan. (Photo by G. Desisto)

CHAPTER 10

The killer "B's"

"I want a boyfriend who will let me wear his varsity jacket."

Anonymous author

Besides having an excellent "A" team during the late seventies and early eighties, URI also had a very good "B" team that could have competed against every college "A" team we played against. The "B" team in rugby terms was the junior varsity team. This team usually consisted of players that had some rugby experience but had better teammates ahead of them in their specific position at the time and also novice players who might have been very talented but did not have enough playing experience to play on the "A" or varsity team. They might have also had some previously injured players trying to make a comeback with the "A" team while competing in a "B" match as a warm-up preparation for their next "A" match.

URI also possessed a "C" team for many years comprised of those athletes who didn't make either of the first two teams. Many rugby teams especially men's clubs had "C" teams. This "C" match was the last match of the day on game day Saturdays and sometimes, we couldn't field a full "C" team so some of the "B" or even "A" team players would participate in this last match after already completing one full rugby match.

This wasn't such a bright idea because beer kegs lined the sidelines nearly every rugby match and after the "A" match was completed, the ruggers started drinking from these lukewarm kegs. This led to some inebriated "A" and "B" team members playing in the "C" match, a dangerous thing to do. I never played a second rugby match during my career; my body couldn't handle it especially due to hamstring issues during matches that were common for me and that made it impossible to run during a second match. I had no desire to play a meaningless "C" match after competing in a highly competitive varsity "A" match. I didn't need the extra chance of a rugby injury either that might sideline me for the next week's opponent.

Over the years, the "B" team built their reputation as the other half of the Rhody Rugby Club. A few times during a season, they had more wins than the "A" team and many of the "regular" "B" players who had no chance or a slim chance of playing on the "A" team, relished this position to be in. Each match to them was just as important as the previous "A" match they had watched as they warmed up on the sidelines and they gave it their best in this very physical, combative, crazy game.

In 1976, after the "A" team posted a 10-2-2 record, the "B" team went undefeated playing against the same opponent's "B" teams. A few of these key ruggers during that fall season were: George, Lenny T, and Reed. These three players also moved up to the "A" side after a season or two and Reed became one of the stars of our sevens team. Other very good "B" ruggers during this time were:

Andy, Chris "Okie" Oakley, Ted, Will, Steve "Cass" Caster, Larry Reinhold, Dave J, Mike Dyer, Ray A, "Boomer", and Cody James.

At some point during one of our seasons, they were nicknamed the "Killer Bees" and they were fun to watch. Many of these players did end up playing for the "A" team for some matches due to graduation, injuries, players not showing up, or they improved and replaced their "A" team counterpart. The "B" team always had more to prove than the "A" team ruggers in practice and matches. I already mentioned that the "B" team also competed in the same special sevens tournaments that the "A" team competed in especially in the New York Sevens college tournaments. In 1978 at the New York Sevens tourney, they swept their opponents and reached the finals to meet the URI "A" team.

Looking back, I think many of those ruggers really wanted a shot at playing against us on that cold, dreary day but it didn't happen. The "A" team was rendered the victory decided upon by our senior club members and the New York tournament committee and officials that I mentioned in a previous chapter. That might have been one rugby match for the URI decade if we had really played against each other. We did provide the "B" team with our trophies because most of us had at least one sevens trophy due to a previous sevens tournament win.

Rugby Club has come a long way

The URI Rugby Club has come a long way since its start seven years ago. The schedule has shifted from amateurish college teams to the experienced city clubs of Boston and Providence. Although the team remains a club sport, enough members have joined to produce three separate teams. The A-side is the most competitive of the teams, posting an 8-2 fall record and a 7-4 spring record. The B-side sports the best record of the club, defeating many A-side opponents and trouncing B-side teams. Their fall and spring records were 9-1 and 8-1-1. The C-side played above a .500 average and provided new players with much experience.

Highlights for the season included play against two excellent foreign teams, the University of Newcastle and an all-star French team. The team also took first place in the New York 7-A-side Tournament in the fall, and placed as runner-up in the prestigious Harvard Sevens for the third year in a row.

Above is a great article concerning the "B" team and their record in 1978 that was featured in the sports section of the 1978 URI yearbook. Some of these ruggers never played for the "A" side but they still played hard at practices and in the matches and enjoyed the total camaraderie of this great game and the social traditions after the matches. The yearbook did make an error when detailing that our club was established in the early seventies. The 1966 Grist yearbook lists the club's beginning as 1966. This past year – 2016, was the fiftieth anniversary of the Rhody Rugby Club.

Two rugby backs that played on the "B" team that stood out over the years in my opinion were Vinnie Patrone and Corie Joseph. Both were excellent Rhode Island high school football players who never played an "A" match for the URI Rugby Club because we had so many other fast or powerful backs but they did stand out in the "B" matches and sometimes in some of our own practices and scrimmages.

Corie Joseph played running back for East Greenwich, a Division II or class "B" team. When Corie played in high school, divisions were based on the total student enrollment. Division I was the highest division and usually represented the better teams in each sport in Rhode Island. The division or "class" that the school was part of didn't matter for some sports such as track, swimming, and wrestling because at the end of the season, they all competed for one state championship. They may have had "class" or "division" championships but only one team was considered the true state champion.

All the other sports each had an individual state champion for every division, very strange in such a small state as Rhode Island. The current system in Rhode Island has changed drastically. Now, schools can compete in different divisions for each sport and schools can move up and down in a division after a few years, depending upon how well they perform in their current division.

I don't know all the rules or policies on how this is set up – but to me, it causes much confusion for athletic directors and coaches for all the schools. It seems this change was made so every team can win a state championship and some schools can "tank" so they stay in a lower division and then they can compete against weaker teams. This is only my opinion, I'm sure many athletic directors and coaches could explain a better reason and would not agree with my opinion. Recently in high school basketball, there is a true state champion and teams from all divisions are seeded and qualify for this tournament based on a special calculated point system.

Corie was voted the best high school football player in Rhode Island in his senior year after scoring the most touchdowns of any other player in the state that year and his team was undefeated. He went on to attend the University of Rhode Island and competed on both the football and track varsity teams. I'm not sure what happened but at some point, he stopped playing football and joined our rugby team. Corie was very fast and scored many touchdowns for the "B" team and he seemed to enjoy this new "game" that we all had recently discovered. He played for a few years and helped the "B" team win many matches.

Vinnie only played for one rugby season and maybe another half of a season. He was also an excellent high school football player who starred for East Providence High School, a Division I school where I went to high school and labored on the track team. Vinnie also competed in track at East Providence and his best events were the 50 and 100 yard dash. (The distances for track events during my high school years were marked in yards and not meters.) He was good in rugby immediately even though he had little experience but most good football players pick up the game of rugby quickly, especially if they played a running back position.

Vinnie and I were friends and lived in the same fraternity – Sigma Nu. He started playing rugby after I had been with the club for a few seasons. Vinnie would have eventually made the "A" team and been an excellent rugger with his size and speed if he had stuck it out for a longer period of time but he thought the match selection officers were biased so he quit the team. I tried to talk him into staying on the team but he would have none of it.

I might have also hurt his chances for making the "A" team. Vinnie played inside center and I played wing so we never went head to head. But anytime I saw him breaking tackles and running past his matching center in practice, I would try to tackle him and make sure he didn't go all the way. Practices and scrimmages were very competitive, and it didn't matter who I played against on my own team. I couldn't let them show me up – it might put me in jeopardy of not playing "A"s for the upcoming weekend – whether they played my position or not.

Vinnie is still remembered in his hometown for scoring four touchdowns against East Providence's main football school rival and enemy – LaSalle Academy, a private school in Providence on one of the Thanksgiving Day special morning games. Thanksgiving Day football games were a long tradition in Rhode Island and this rivalry at the time in the early seventies was one of the longest in the state.

Vinnie and I are in the photo below featured in my East Providence High School senior yearbook with some of the 1973 Indoor Track team members. Vinnie is in the middle row and was a junior at the time and I am in front of him in the bottom row – both highlighted with circles. Long hair and large side burns were in. We looked very young. (Photo by Richard Jezierney/Kathi Kelly)

Below is a Harvard Sevens program bracket from one of these tournaments we entered in the late seventies. The URI "B" team always played well in sevens tournaments probably because they played against the "A" team during practices in preparation. They also had their share of good wins in many of these matches. Other men's clubs as well as college teams also brought their second team.

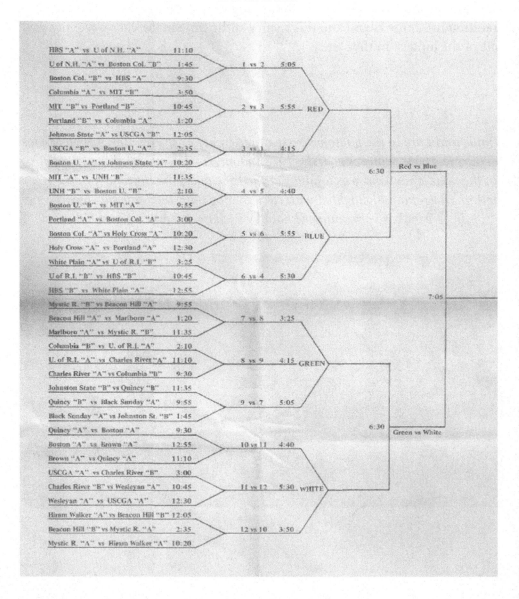

CHAPTER 11

Olympic rugby history, URI rugby history and the Glue

"There is a history in all men's lives."

William Shakespeare – Famous British poet and playwright.

Rugby's original entry in the Olympic Games was in 1900 and the game had a powerful backer – a French aristocrat, historian, and educator named Baron de Coubertin. Baron de Coubertin was the founder of the modern Olympics and was a devoted sports enthusiast who thought physical education and intelligence could have saved his country from military destruction in wars and battles in the late 1800s.

He also admired the ethics, competitiveness, and team spirit of sports and helped to establish rugby as a sport in France. Rugby was introduced to the Olympics in those 1900 Paris Games, and the home team won. Baron de Coubertin who also played and refereed rugby football was elected into the World Rugby Hall of Fame in 2007.

This sport did not repeat at the 1904 Games in St. Louis but returned four years later in London, where the home squad was defeated by Australia. When Baron de Coubertin left the presidency of the International Olympic Committee (IOC) in 1925, rugby left the Games.

While outside the Olympics, rugby gained in popularity around the world and recently in the United States. It is still more popular outside the U.S. for three simple reasons:

- It's an inexpensive sport with minimal equipment and similar to soccer so many countries can play this game and develop national teams.

- The U.S. has American football which is a derivative of rugby and currently is the most popular American sport, outdistancing baseball, the old American pastime. Imagine if American football players played rugby – what a national team we would have!

- The U.S. has an abundance of other sports for children and adults to choose from as compared to most countries, especially the smaller countries.

In 1996, the International Rugby Board (IRB) was officially recognized by the IOC and the following year, the sport became professional, exactly 100 years after the first league was founded in England.

In 2009, an IOC committee decided to add rugby, both men and women's teams once again to the Olympic program at the 2016 Games. These Games were played in Rio de Janeiro but only featured the rugby sevens version, the version of rugby that the URI Rugby Football Club excelled at. Rugby's fifteen-a-side version was a medal sport at the four Summer Games in the early nineteen-hundreds only and the United States was the last Olympic Rugby champion in 1924.

Qualification for these Olympic Games was similar to the qualification process that occurs with soccer. Not every country was able to participate in the actual 2016 Olympic Games.

The men's Rugby Sevens Tournament consisted of 12 countries and Brazil the home team automatically qualified for this event. Other qualifications included the 2014-2015 Sevens World Series and the 2015 regional rugby unions had an Olympic qualification event as well, with one team from each region as a qualifier. The final berth was a "winner takes all" tournament with the champion obtaining the final spot in the Rugby Games.

The women's Rugby Sevens Tournament also consisted of 12 countries competing for the Gold Medal in the suburb of Deodoro. One automatic qualification place went to the host team Brazil and the remaining 11 spots available had a few different paths similar to the men's route that determined which team would receive a spot in the Olympic Tournament. These various paths included tournaments or match standings such as the 2014-2015 Women's Sevens World Series, a top ranking in the 2015 Regional Association Women's Sevens Championships, and one last spot from the final Olympic Qualification Tournament. The USA rugby squads had to play well in order to qualify for these 2016 Rugby Games.

URI Rugby History

The URI Rugby Club was founded in 1966 at the University of Rhode Island and there is little or no information or statistics on how they fared up until the mid-seventies when I played for this club. This is when the team established itself as one of the better fifteen-a-side teams in New England, against both college and men's club teams in these standard rugby matches. In seven-a-side rugby, URI was recognized as a powerhouse in the East and competed nationally.

The URI "GRIST" yearbook of 1966 dedicated a page to this newly discovered sport at the university. Below are some of the clippings from this yearbook.

1966 marked the birth of another sport here at Kingston — it reminds one of football with no regard for rules — Rugby.

Rugby is a rough sport with a complicated method of scoring — related to the nature of the kick — and fifteen men per team run around for a two uninterrupted half-hour periods, with neither padding nor substitutions.

The game, which originated in England when an excited soccer player disregarded the rules and ran with the ball, is played on a field a little larger than 100 yards, and is played with a ball which is a little more portly than the classic pigskin.

The URI team, playing a brief schedule, fared rather well against the Brown team and Holy Cross. Next year should be great.

	URI	OPPONENT
NY over 30's	12	12
	30	0
Brown C team	0	0
	9	0
Rutgers	0	14
Holy Cross	5	3

The URI Rugby Club did have some moderate success in the early seventies from 1971 through 1974 when they scheduled mostly college teams and some "B" team clubs or schools. Butch Paranzino was one of the organizers and captains of these teams who played scrum-half and also wrote some of the articles that were in the "Cigar". Butch played for many years with the Providence RFC after he graduated.

Matt Kohler was also part of these teams that competed with Butch and other students who started playing with the Rhody Rugby Club in 1971 and he ended his career in 1976 (five year school plan). Matt was tall and thin and very athletic; he played wing forward or second row in the scrum. I remember playing with Matt during my first full rugby year – 1976.

In the photo above from the "74" yearbook, this rugger ran well in his jean shorts. I can't imagine playing in these. Maybe he forgot his regular rugby shorts for that match. (Photo by Yearbook staff)

One of Butch's articles (The "Cigar" misspelled his name.) concerning a match that took place on October 29, 1971.

URI rugby club surprises Wesleyan with 43-0 shutout

By Butch Parenzino

The University of Rhode Island rugby club traveled to Amherst, Mass., last Saturday to meet Wesleyan College, and returned to Kingston with an unexpected 43-0 victory.

Wesleyan has been recognized as a strong and established rugby club, and although the Rhode Island "A" squad was matched with Wesleyan's second team, the game was expected to be an even contest.

This was not the case. URI completely outclassed Wesleyan from the initial kickoff.

Merlin O'Keefe broke the scoring ice after just a few minutes of play, as he pounced on a loose ball in the end zone. Shortly after, scrum-half Butch Parenzino scampered 30 yards for the second score and Dan Callahan added two points with the conversion.

Dan was the brightest offensive star for the Rams, as he personally accounted for 23 points. His valuable toe added 19 points to the scoreboard via five touchdown conversions for 10 points and three penalty field goals for nine points.

Dan also managed a breakaway run from his fullback position late in the second half for the final touchdown of the game. Other players who contributed to the scoring were Cliff Hightower, who crossed the goal-line twice, and fleet-footed Dave Steckler.

The rugby club displayed a hard-nose defense that broke the back of the Wesleyan team. As it turned out, the contest was not a true match for the URI ruggers, but it did instill a great deal of confidence in the team.

This confidence will be a definite asset this weekend, as the rugby club will send two full teams to Fairfield College. Fairfield is considered very strong and the result of this match should be a truer indication of the rugby club's talent.

The next home game for the URI ruggers is November 6, by the varsity soccer field.

"The History of women's rugby in the United States can be traced back to three teams that existed in 1972 – The Colorado State University Hookers at Fort Collins; the University of Colorado, at Boulder; and the University of Illinois, at Champaign. During the mid-1970s, women's teams began to spring up on college campuses across the United States. As those players graduated, they went on to set up teams near cities and urban centers. At that time, there was only one division for all women's rugby."

U.S. Women's Rugby Foundation website

The URI women's rugby club is becoming more popular and competitive since they started playing in the early eighties. In 2007, they captured a national college title by completing their 2006 fall season undefeated and that earned them an invitation to the New England Rugby Football Union's Division IV club team championship. That team then went on to play for the national title in the spring. The Rams traveled to Philadelphia and beat Ursinus College 36 to 5 for the national title. Like other club athletes at URI, the women's rugby team pay a fee to play and they organize and participate in fund-raisers to cover team expenses, including equipment, and travel.

The coaches for that successful season were: Head Coach Nate Godfrey, a Narragansett, Rhode Island resident at the time who played rugby with the Providence Club, and a few other veteran rugby players and Assistant Coaches – Brian Moore, Skip Barry, Mike DeGiulio (Mike played for URI for a few seasons.), and Patrick Jaquet. Currently, the women's team competes in Division I, having moved up to the top division over the last few years.

The URI men's college team is also having much success while competing in the New England Collegiate Rugby Conference – Division II, but neither men's nor women's team compete against non-college teams or in non-college tournaments. This is a much more organized and safer format than when I played and makes much better sense with distinct divisions based on location, skill level, size of the school, etc. and colleges playing against other colleges only.

Some colleges and universities that compete in Division I rugby now offer various types of scholarships. They also provide travel, equipment, uniforms, etc. that are paid for by the school and they are fully sanctioned by USA Rugby and some women's teams are considered NCAA varsity programs.

So much has changed since I played rugby at URI with our wide open schedule of matches and tournaments against any rugby team that would play us.

The men's club finished as runners-up in their college rugby conference (fifteen-a-side) three of the past four seasons but in the fall of 2015, URI took first place. Tries from Alex Sabitoni and Darryl Brooks, as well as a strong kicking performance from fly-half Anthony Kennedy, enabled the Rams to post a 15-7 win over the University of Vermont and a conference title in the last match of the season. This win also avenged their only loss on their schedule to Vermont, and the URI Rugby Club qualified for the USA Rugby National College Tournament (Division II) – consisting of the top sixteen college teams in the country in that division. The next set of matches was played on Founders Field in Pittsburgh.

Rhody beat their first opponent – Oswego State University out of New York – by a score of 58 to 17. They lost to their next opponent – University of Wisconsin Whitewater – who averaged over sixty points per match during their fall season and at the time was ranked second in the nation. That made URI one of the top eight collegiate rugby teams in their division in the United States and a final ranking of fifth in the country – not bad for the smallest state in the union. Below is an article posted on the club's Facebook site and a travel photo courtesy of one of their fans. The coaches for this successful season were Head Coach: Warren Boothman, and Assistant Coaches: Mike Traynor, Skip Barry, and Chris Gray. All of these coaches played for the Providence Rugby Football men's club during their competitive rugby days.

"Rhody Rugby concluded its season on Sunday in Pittsburgh after advancing to the National Quarterfinals. This past season has been the most successful season in recent years for the club. URI finished the season as Champions of the New England Collegiate Rugby Conference and was able to beat SUNY Oswego by a score of 58-17 in the National Playoffs. They then faced the University of Wisconsin – Whitewater, who are ranked 2nd in the nation. While Rhody was unable to come out on top, they gave Wisconsin a very strong showing and were only narrowly beaten by a score of 31-21."

URI Rugby Club Facebook website

Below is the current Rhody Rugby Team prior to their visit to the Nationals. Head coach Warren Boothman is in the bottom row holding a rugby ball, far right. (Photo by Kathy Liguori)

One of the men's ruggers who graduated from URI in 2007 was Kyle Marshall. Kyle started playing rugby as a freshman for this Division II club. He is a Rhode Island native who played various sports at Narragansett High School but turned to rugby in college. Kyle was a Wildlife and Conservation Biology major at the university, who mixed sports with academics during his four years.

Kyle continued playing rugby after he graduated for the Boston Rugby Club, a great New England men's team and he also coached rugby in his spare time. In 2010, Kyle was selected to play for the U.S. National Rugby Sevens team which is the non-traditional version of rugby that URI had excelled at in the seventies and eighties.

Kyle's rugby career allowed him to travel and compete in various rugby tournaments and matches around the world. The last I heard, Kyle was employed as a Biology teacher at a high school in Randolph, Massachusetts and is still mixing it up with other ruggers on the pitch. Kyle would have fit in nicely with our sevens team.

The Glue

"It doesn't matter who scores the points, it's who can get the ball to the scorer."

Larry Bird – Retired NBA Indiana Pacers team president and Boston Celtics American Basketball Hall of Fame player.

Rob Calissi was one of the captains of the URI Rugby Club and the "glue" that kept the team together when I played. He handled many club roles and played fly-half for the team. Rob scheduled many of the matches, prepared the field for the Saturday afternoon contests, designed and ordered our special URI Rugby Team jackets, and with Barry Richard's help and original design work brought new, updated jerseys to the team. He also arranged post party locations working with the other club committee members and ordered the kegs of beer from the package store that gave the largest discount, etc.

He was devoted to the team, both on and off the rugby field. Rob excelled at both offense and defense and outplayed his opposing fly-half most of the matches we played. He was an intense player who left everything on the pitch even when he had injuries that would have kept other players from competing that particular day. I would have to say that Rob was the "guy" who helped us achieve a higher level of rugby than any of us could have imagined with his never-say-die attitude and his elusive running and great passing skills, especially in those special sevens matches.

In some of these tournaments, we were matched against some of the top sevens teams (all men's clubs) in the East such as Boston Rugby Club, Black Sunday, Beacon Hill, Old Blue, Hartford Wanderers, Old Gold, and Mystic River. Rob always made sure the backs received the ball quickly after the scrum-half delivered him the ball so we could take advantage of the open field; he was a playmaker on the pitch. At wing, I was the last rugger to touch the ball when the backs ran their offense and Rob who played fly-half was considered the quarterback of the team.

Rob was one of those team players that made everybody else better than what they were, including me. I never played football so the tackling part of rugby did not come easy to me. I was fast so offense was no problem – I scored tries, but when I first started playing rugby, my defense was somewhat suspect. Luckily, I was usually matched against other wingers who were my size and not that physical either.

After playing many practice scrimmages and a few matches, I learned to tackle from watching both Rob and "Dirty" Harry. They would hit the opposing players while on defense with such skill and force even though both athletes were five foot nine and weighed about 175 pounds, I figured out that I could do the same thing. **It's not the size of the dog in the fight; it's the size of the fight in the dog** and one match I distinctly remember against Boston University is when the light bulb went on for me.

Early in the match, I found myself one on one with my opposing wing who had the ball and was coming right at me. If I didn't stop him, he would easily score the first try of the match. I hadn't had much time to think about it so I ran as fast as I could directly at him and stuck my head into the ribs of this average size wing. He went down very hard and lost the ball and I was still standing with no sign of wear or tear. I didn't hurt myself and it felt great.

Nobody explained to me how to tackle opposing players (Many of our team played football and some thought I had this background too.) but I witnessed it close up observing Rob, Harry, and some of my other teammates. After that BU match that we won, I actually enjoyed playing defense almost as much as offense and making sure no back got past me whether it was my matching wing or one of the opposing middle backs who beat one of my teammates. Speed helps on defense too – the faster I charged an opponent and made a direct hit, the harder he fell.

When Rob left URI, he played for the White Plains Rugby Club and the URI Old Boys in sevens tournaments and played competitive rugby for a few more years including regional select sides – up until he was 40 years old. He traveled to England, France, Hong Kong, South Korea, and some other areas outside the United States over those years competing in this game that predated American football. He even dabbled in "Old Boys" fifteens rugby after that because he loved this game so much.

Rob also played football on Sundays for a few years after playing rugby on Saturdays when he played for White Plains. Rob played quarterback for a semi-pro football team in the New York area. I'm not sure how he did this for those years but he told me his secret after his career was over – he didn't run much on Sunday. **Instead, he threw the ball often and he saved his running for rugby.**

Ted Kiley was the "B" team version of Rob. He served on the various club committees and held a few different officer positions while spending many hours working for the club without being paid. He was a large part of the "B" team's great seasons during his playing days. Ted also played fly-half.

The article below (only a small portion of it) was written after a Cigar reporter interviewed Rob concerning the financial support that the URI Rugby Club received each year.

by Gary Grabowski
Cigar Sports Staff

Scrapping, scratching and digging are three things that continously take place on the field in a rugby game. For the participant, play is demanding. For the URI rugby club things are somewhat different.

The scrapping, scratching and digging for the Rams begins before the season even starts in the form of raising money to support the club. Because the team is a club sport, it receives only a small sum of money from the athletic department. The money appropriated ($500.00) is for both the fall and spring seasons and goes toward expenses for the B and C squads as well as the A team.

All money raised or appropriated goes toward union dues, as the Rams are part of the rugby union; tournament entry fees, paying officials and for parties among other things.

Yes, parties are an expense which must be met because in rugby, it is tradition for the home club to provide refreshments after the game.

Anybody can play for the URI rugby club. There are no eligibility rules or age limitations for a college club, which the Rams are. Eligibility rules do exist for a college team.

"We do get a lot of players from the area as well as the school,"

Rob and I in this photo were discussing strategy prior to a URI Rugby alumni match held in the early eighties. Of course, we won that day, beating the younger URI ruggers. (Photo by L. O'Neil)

CHAPTER 12

Everything else

"Show me a good loser and I will show you a loser."

Paul Newman – American screen actor, director, professional race car driver, and Oscar winner.

Road Warriors

The URI Rugby Football Club played many road matches over the years during the seventies and early eighties and we always provided our own transportation to all of these matches. This meant we traveled in a caravan of cars and trucks to the away matches throughout New England and sometimes much further.

Never mind that most of these vehicles that we drove were not the newest or in the best condition because most of us were students or recent URI graduates with low paying jobs and a new car was not one of our budget priorities during this time.

Many of these vehicles could have broken down on the road at any time but we were all very young and payed no attention to those things that might occur with our shaky transportation vehicles.

Most of us had very little extra money to spend on automobiles during our undergrad years, so many of us became very creative with our workaround "fixes" for our older, problem automobiles. I broke two door handles on my Ford Pinto one year and rather than paying money at an auto store for door handles, I duct taped pieces of wood to the remnants of the two door handles and they lasted until the next auto inspection date.

Okie, who played one of the "B" center positions during my URI rugby days, always carried a hockey stick in the trunk of his car in case his car didn't start. He had a faulty starter and he would pull out his hockey stick, open the hood, and use the hockey stick to tap the starter a few times and then he could start his car again and continue driving to the match.

There were a few flat tires during our travels up and back to rugby matches but I don't remember any major breakdowns that cost the team a few players for a special match or tournament. We did leave a rugger back in Kingston a few times when a teammate had a late night out the previous evening and overslept or disappeared and missed the designated time when the Rhody Rugby Team caravan had to depart from campus to make the matches on time.

If the missing player was a key member of the "A" team, some of us might try to call that player (no cell phones then of course) or even stop at his dorm or off-campus residence to see if we could find and deliver this player to the match on time. Many older students lived in rented houses far from campus in one of the nearby small towns.

Sometimes, these "search parties" could lead to an embarrassing moment or two if that player was with his girlfriend or a girl that he recently met at a bar or party the previous night. Mick was one of these players who fell into that category – he had a few different girlfriends and as I explained in a previous chapter, he enjoyed parties and socializing. Mick was an excellent scrum forward – tall and strong. He was picked for the New England Select Side once or twice during his rugby career with the URI Club.

There were other times that some of the drivers became lost while traveling to these away matches due to various reasons. GPS devices didn't exist in cars in those years and cell phones and the Internet did not exist either. Our tools that helped us meet our game time start deadline for our many matches were: written directions, paper road maps, word of mouth, or just our good memories. These simple tools alone helped us get from point A to point B. The "A" game was always the first match on Saturday so the "B" and "C" team ruggers could show up late – and this did happen but the "A" team couldn't be late. We could always fill in with a "B" player but we hated to miss a key "A" player on match day. There were no substitutions in rugby as I explained previously so we could not substitute late team members into any match.

I can vividly remember one match against the Harvard Business School RFC – we had four or five "A" team ruggers traveling in one car and we were very late. I don't remember how much time the referee gave a team before they started the match but soon these players would not be able to play in this first match - so the driver actually stopped the car in the breakdown lane of Storrow Drive, somewhat close to the rugby field. Then all but the driver ran across the road, avoiding the heavy traffic, jumping a fence or two and then proceeded directly onto the pitch with no stretching or warming up. It was something to see.

Most of our matches were in Massachusetts, Connecticut, or New York and some of the team members lived in these states so missing or wrong directions to these road matches didn't always pose a problem. We all eventually made it to our destination.

The biggest and most dangerous problem with our means of travel came after the match and after the postgame party. Who was responsible enough in the various vehicles we drove up to the match – and who hadn't had very much to drink during the party – to drive the other ruggers back to Kingston. Usually, it was also late evening when we headed back to campus so the drive home was more complicated at that time in the darkness especially if it was raining or there was other inclement weather.

We didn't have any major accidents during my away game travels but there was one "roll-over" after an away match on Route 2 in Rhode Island just past "Allie's Donuts" and miraculously, nobody was hurt and I was not part of this group. Allie's is still there today – doing better than ever, a Rhode Island local tradition. You've probably seen that old commercial on television or the advertisement on the Wheaties cereal box in the local market – "Wheaties, the Breakfast of Champions". The URI ruggers always stopped at Allie's when traveling north to away matches and bought some of these special, home-made donuts and small cartons of milk or juice "to go" and dined while driving. I wouldn't recommend this type of breakfast before engaging in any running sport but that's exactly what we did when I played for URI and it didn't seem to bother any of us – **"Allie's, the Breakfast of the URI Rugby Club"**.

The police arrived at the scene a few minutes later but nobody was arrested. The drinking and driving laws were somewhat lax back then and I guess because nobody was hurt in the accident and no other car was involved – the police might have looked the other way and given these college students a break. The story I heard was that the driver fell asleep and the rest of the passengers in the car were already sleeping – visions of the Chevy Chase movie – "National Lampoon's Vacation". No harm, no foul! The Rhody Ruggers were very lucky that day and it had nothing to do with a big win.

The farthest our rugby team traveled for a match was Florida for a few Spring Break matches. I played in only one of these scheduled rugby games in 1978 – we played a college team from Fort Lauderdale. Some drove their own cars but the majority of players, thirteen total including myself drove down to Florida in a rented Winnebago. We had ample time to make this match but a late snowstorm arrived during our scheduled "takeoff" and this alone could have led to a disastrous and dangerous accident but it didn't.

Our first stop once the baker's dozen ruggers boarded was the local liquor store and market. At the liquor store, we bought many cases of the most inexpensive beer on sale that day (Our selection was probably Pabst, Narragansett, or Black Label – we were not fussy as student beer drinkers.) and at the market, we bought only bread, peanut butter, jelly, and a few large bags of potato chips and off we went. Only the serious and non-drinking ruggers were allowed to drive – this was the only rule we had on this trip.

Rob had driven home to New York the previous day so we had one more stop to pick up Rob and then we could drive straight through to Florida, stopping only for more food or gas whenever either ran out. It was still snowing when we stopped in front of Rob's house in Yonkers with the Winnebago and surprise! Rob and his mom boarded the Winnebago with fifteen small lasagna dishes covered in aluminum foil – still hot and fresh out of the oven. The timing was perfect. Rob's mother was a fantastic Italian cook and some of us had the opportunity to enjoy his mom's cooking previously when we visited his family before the New York Sevens tournament, including her special chocolate cake. What a treat!

Along the route we encountered a few issues such as a blocked toilet inside the Winnebago and we did eventually stop at a gas station and someone figured out what had to be done. The rest of the drive was much more pleasant after the one toilet on the Winnebago was fixed.

We stopped at a fraternity party when we were close to Fort Lauderdale because one of the Rhody Ruggers had a cousin in this fraternity. (I'm not sure what school in Florida we visited that day.) The party was just beginning to get busy and that was fun but we had to leave the party to make sure we made it to Fort Lauderdale for at least one day of rest and sightseeing before the big match.

Below is the Florida rugby match advertisement for one of our farthest away matches that was advertised in the "Cigar", a week or so prior to the match.

Injuries

Rugby players have their share of injuries especially when rugby players don't wear helmets or pads and tackling is a large part of the game. When I played, we did use a "gum-shield" or "mouthpiece" for American football readers and some players wore a cup to protect the groin area. Today, some rugby players wear lightweight skull caps used to cover and protect their ears, primarily for scrum players and some shirts have tiny shoulder pads in them – but still no real protection.

I had a few minor injuries during my rugby tenure but nothing serious. I received about 10 to 12 stitches over my right eyebrow after a night home match, various hamstring pulls, and I had thumb and finger problems for most of my career. This, including a few small finger breaks, hardly noticeable now other than my left curved small index finger. I used a great amount of athletic tape on my fingers over the years due to the continuous hand grabbing and tackling on defensive plays to stop the forward progress of my opponents. I remember an away match at Yale when too much tape cost us the match.

It was a close match and towards the end, JTags made a nice move to fake his matching center and the wing opposite me was forced to then go after JTags. I was left alone on the outside pitch area and JTags lofted a perfect pass to me on the run as I was in full gallop with nobody in front of me and about 25 or 35 meters left to the goal area for an easy try and the lead.

Both my right and left thumbs were wrapped up so heavy that day – I bobbled the ball a few times and then totally dropped it for a knock on as I fell to the ground in a heap. A few minutes later, the whistle blew and I blew the match. We laughed about it at the party and the whole next week, I never taped both thumbs again no matter how messed up they were – they are important to help catch the ball.

We scheduled a home, night match one season under the lights on the football practice field against a men's city club – Springfield RFC. Three of us were injured in that match. I was the first casualty – I hit one of my opponents with my head after aiming at his upper chest but instead of hitting the target area, I missed and hit the side of his head with the sharp blow. I didn't feel that bad after the contact but then, I noticed the blood on my shirt – it was pouring out from a large slice or cut right over my right eyebrow. I played for another minute or two and then walked off the pitch. The blood was not stopping.

A friend drove me to the local hospital and I had a towel on the cut so the bleeding had subsided some but I needed more than a few stitches that evening and had to wait in the Emergency Room for the next available doctor.

It was a busy night at South County Hospital. About twenty minutes later, Cody came into the same hospital with a hyperextended elbow. Next, "Cass" arrived at the hospital and he had a few chipped or broken teeth and a mouth injury.

The nurse looked at all of us and said, "You must have really gotten beaten by the better team tonight in your game." "No, not really," I told her. "We killed them, even playing short two players at the end of the game." Cody kept battling and never came out of the game until the match ended. He just didn't use his bad left arm and kept it on his side. They were a very physical team but we outran them, put up too many points on the board, and played excellent defense. All of our injuries occurred while we were playing defense. That's rugby.

A few other more serious rugby injuries that I knew about that had occurred beyond the twisted ankles, bruised knees, pulled hamstrings, black eyes, etc. were:

- Mike Tagliardi cracked a testicle while making a low tackle in a match against the University of Connecticut but luckily, men have two of these. He continued playing at URI but always wore an athletic cup over his groin area after this mishap. He did enjoy having children after he was married so I guess the cup worked fine.

- Dave Dimeo, one of the early "A" backs I played with, tackled an opposing player on the sidelines while scrimmaging against the "B" team in a practice session and went to the ground hard. When he stood up, he was dizzy and had some blurred vision. He went to his family eye doctor the next day and was told he needed to wear glasses forever. He stopped playing for the team.

- Reed Reynolds lost his two front teeth after a hard tackle in a match against Mystic RFC and he was wearing a mouthpiece. I think he stayed in the match for a few more plays and still made an appearance at the party. He continued playing rugby for URI and later for the Providence RFC and now wears two front false teeth that are built similar to a retainer. He can easily remove them if necessary. He attended a Halloween party one year while still a student as Leon Spinks the great boxer who was also missing his two front teeth. The accident sometimes came in handy for Reed.

- A few teammates in the scrum sometimes would pop out or dislocate their shoulders during a practice or a match and then have one of their own teammates pop it back in for them. Wes and Tats were two of our players that had this little issue but it never stopped them from playing in a match while at URI.

- Paul Seddon in a sevens match against the Mystic River RFC, during one of the Harvard Sevens tournaments, suffered a serious concussion after a hard tackle and had to leave the match. In those days, there was no legitimate test and few concerns about concussions but if a player looked or appeared groggy during a physical confrontation during a match – he was checked out. The referee or his own team members would then hold up a few fingers and ask him how many fingers were showing. A few questions might also have been asked such as: Where are you? What's your name? Paul flunked this unscientific test and we played the rest of the match with only six players. We still won that match and advanced to the finals of the tournament that year.

Below is a portion of an article that was in the 'Cigar' on May 5, 1976 that mentioned this specific incident as well as some information about the team and how we competed during that sevens tourney. This was my first rugby sevens tournament and it was exciting.

Ruggers close out season impressively

The URI rugby club team finished their regular season with three straight shutouts as they captured six of their final seven contests.

But the highlight of the season, if you can imagine anything overshadowing a great season like the ruggers had, came this past Sunday. Rhody's ruggers finished second in the 36-team Harvard seven's tournament in Cambridge.

In the seven's tournament, there are only seven men on the field as opposed to the usual 15. All the rest of the rules are the same. It proved to fit the Rams style perfectly as they took advantage of their speed and hustle to become the talk of the tournament.

Rhody was paired against all the top rugby teams in New England. They downed four straight opponents; 14-0 over Charles River, 19-12 over Old Gold of Boston, 26-0 over Beacon Hill, and 10-0 over Black Sunday of Boston.

These four victories placed the Rams in the semi-finals against Mystic of Boston. It was in this game that Rhody really won the hearts of all the fans present. Winning by a score of 6-0, the Rams Paul Seddon, who was exceptional all day, suffered a head injury and was forced to leave the game.

Under the rules, no substitution during a game is allowed and the Rams were forced to play with only six men. Rhody somehow managed enough pride and amazingly even added another score to advance to the finals by way of a 10-0 victory. It was their fifth straight victory and fourth shutout.

139

Coaches – Who Needs Them

One of the most significant aspects concerning the URI Rugby Club during my playing days had to be the absence of an official rugby coach. I have never given this much thought over the years but while working on this non-fiction sports book project, I've come to realize this was a major disadvantage and possible drawback for most of us who played various sports since we were in grade school. It probably also contributed to some of our losses, especially in our early years when many of us were still learning the game. We did play without coaches in pickup games of basketball, baseball, football, etc. in some of our backyards, nearby fields, and streets where we lived when we were younger. But for all other organized sports that existed in our town recreation leagues, middle schools, high schools, etc., we had coaches.

These coaches, whether we thought they were good or bad, taught us how to play the specific game, established the starting lineups and substitutions for the players, and controlled the whole environment including practice times, team policies, etc. Not so with the URI Rugby Team that played all their matches without a coach on the sidelines and played a game that most of us had no familiarity with until we came to URI.

The first rugby practice I participated in behind Keaney Gymnasium felt like another pickup game that I played in when I was younger; local neighborhood kids getting together and having some simple athletic fun. Nobody sat out in those early childhood pickup games even if we had an uneven number of players. If the team numbers weren't equal, then one team played with less competitors but usually that team consisted of a few of the better or stronger players to make the teams equal in skill level and allow a balanced and competitive game.

Arguments hardly occurred in those pickup games other than the typical team vs. team discussions such as: what occurred first – a foul or a travel, was the home run in fair territory or not, did the ball carrier get touched "down" with both hands by the defensive player, etc. There were no referees in these unorganized sandlot games either; at least in our rugby matches, we had a referee. If not, those matches would have been very dangerous, out of control, ugly battles due to the physicality of the game.

When I look back at my rugby days on the fields at the URI campus and across various college and men's club fields throughout New England, I realize most rugby teams that we played against had coaches, especially the Ivy League college teams and of course all the men's club teams.

Today, both men's and women's rugby clubs at URI have more than two or three official coaches and these clubs compete in an official college division with a designated format. These teams also have a chance to participate in a national championship if they do well in their respective division playoffs.

Our accomplishments as a highly competitive rugby program with a difficult match schedule prepared by ourselves and the numerous wins in the seventies and early eighties, especially in the sevens tournaments is a feat in itself. We achieved all of this without having coaches by our side drawing up plays, arguing bad referee calls, changing game strategy at half-time if things were not going well, etc. Plus, I don't remember any rugger being cussed out or embarrassed by any of our player/coaches on our team for a missed tackle or a bonehead play, etc. that happens frequently with real coaches in sports. We all got along very well without a coach and we supported each other in the difficult matches and losses.

We also had no statistician keeping track of tries, tackles, assists, or conversions so individuals were not featured in our rugby club – it was the team that counted for wins and losses only. Many players in the pack hardly ever carried the ball more than a few meters or came close to scoring a try but they were still a large part of our team's success and I'm sure they enjoyed watching any of the backs score a try or stop a try with a great tackle.

Bob Hoder did help us with some coaching when he had some free time and a few of the veteran ruggers had coaching roles but for the most part **– there was no Rhode Island Rugby coach and somehow it worked for us!**

Controversy

"In Spring of 1979, the Barbarians also established themselves as a 7's powerhouse. They had won the Harvard Business School 7's in 1978 and were invited to the National Invitational 7's Championships in Hartford in June of 1979. It should be pointed out that during this period of time, one of the great "drifters" to float through Colorado came to the Barbarians by way of Japan. Shinichi Nakamura arrived and asked if he could play...The 7's team of Sean Edris, Milt Bennett, Mike Williams, Chris Hines, Lenny Wineland, and Mark Conley **defeated the University of Rhode Island 12 to 10 in the final match to establish the Barbos as a national 7's power.**"

Denver Barbarians RFC website

In 1979, we played the Denver Barbarians RFC – a dominant men's club in sevens and fifteen-a-side rugby for a national sevens championship match held in Hartford, Connecticut in June. We had both advanced to the finals of this special tournament against other teams that had also qualified for these matches.

We beat the Connecticut Bushwackers 30 to 6, Virginia Polytechnic 24 to 12, and another New England sevens rival – Hartford RFC with a score of 12 to 6. These teams must have won a previous national sevens qualifier tournament somewhere in the country because this tournament was by invitation only. Denver had beaten us in the Harvard Business Sevens rugby final the previous year so we knew we were up against a great men's team.

It was mostly a defensive battle from what I remember on that very hot, summer afternoon. The stupid thing about this match that I also remember was that the URI Rugby Club only wore one type of rugby jersey that was made of a heavy type of clothing material that was geared for the cooler weather. Most of our matches were played during the spring and fall and heat was not an issue. It would have been great and much more practical and efficient to wear a thinner, short-sleeved rugby jersey to help cope with the heat during this early summer tournament. No such luck but that was our own fault. I'm sure that Denver had a "summer" rugby version jersey and wore it during these important matches where every little edge counted. I did remove my mouthpiece that day to help offset some of the heat and make breathing easier without it while running up and down the pitch.

The match details elude me and I don't have any newspaper highlights or game summary clippings to know what other teams were in this national tournament or who scored the tries and conversions but I know we were beating Denver with very little time left in the match. One highlight of my playing career occurred in that same match. It was a defensive play that you hardly ever see in a rugby match but it can happen and I pulled it off during this championship final.

It was early in the second half and one of the Denver ruggers somehow ran past a few of our players and towards the goal area at the corner of the right side of the pitch. I was playing my usual left wing position so I hurried over to try to stop the Denver opponent from getting into the goal area but he was already in. Luckily, he had not touched the ball down for the try and he then tried to continue towards the middle of the goal area so the conversion kick would be easy after touching the ball down. Evidently, in his decision to provide for an easier conversion kick, he didn't see me charging him from the opposite corner.

As he prepared to touch the ball down for the actual try, I lowered my stance and hit him perfectly straight on and at the same time grabbed the rugby ball. With both of us in a standing position and no try scored yet, somehow, I wrestled the ball from him and then touched the ball down in the goal area for a Rhody drop kick at our own goal line, twenty-two meters out. No try was scored!

I had never seen this happen in any match I participated in or watched and nobody ever took a try away from me in the goal area. If it was too difficult to touch the ball down in the middle of the goal area with opposing players close to me, I would touch the ball down wherever I could. Four points and a try was much better than no points and no try even though the conversion kick might be much more difficult kicking from a corner of the pitch; a simple rule for any rugby wing.

We were still leading in this tight match when Paul T, our full-back for that match, tackled one of the Denver players by the back of his jersey but the rugger did not go to the ground. Instead, somehow, Paul drove this same rugger into another Denver player who was in the vicinity trying to start a maul and the two teammates hit heads. Both players went to the ground hard and one was bleeding quite profusely from a head cut. The referee blew his whistle to stop the play as Paul, still standing, watched the two players try to recover.

The next thing we knew both competitors left the pitch and Denver substituted two new, fresh ruggers to replace the supposedly injured players. One of the ruggers did not seem that hurt – the one that was not bleeding – but he was also allowed to be replaced. Rob, our captain, tried to argue our point – were both players really injured or was this just a ploy to get two fresh runners into the match and take advantage of our tired, exhausted team? An obvious advantage was having substitutes in any sevens match. The last time we lost an injured team member in a sevens rugby match a few years ago – we had to finish the match short one player. I don't think any of us knew that the rules had even changed.

A few minutes later, Denver did score a try and connected on the easy two-point conversion kick. The match ended not too long after Denver's last try with the score 12 to 10 and Denver won the match. I still don't understand what happened on that substitution call and was that second player really hurt enough to be ruled out of the match and when did the injured player rule change? Denver is a great team but I do question that referee's decision especially with both competitors being replaced. I'm sure nobody wanted to see a college team beat a men's club in this national rugby tournament and we had no coach or any other rugby representative to argue any of what went down at the end of the match.

I played for the University of Rhode Island in eleven major rugby sevens tournaments and we made the finals in eight or nine of those tournaments. Not bad for a self-coached, novice group of college ruggers and a sevens team that changed personnel every few years due to graduation.

This article was in "The Providence Journal" newspaper after that national defeat by the Denver Barbarians in June 1979. There were some very good sevens clubs in that special tournament. They were all men's clubs from what I remember – except us.

URI ruggers defeated in tourney final, 12-10

Special to the Journal-Bulletin

WEST HARTFORD, Conn. — The University of Rhode Island rugby team won three matches before dropping a 12-10 decision to Denver yesterday in the National Invitational Seven Rugby Tournament.

The Rams defeated the Connecticut Bushwackers, 30-0, scored a 24-12 victory over Virginia Polytech and defeated Hartford, 12-7.

URI's invitation came as a result of its victory in the Harvard Seven Tournament.

Best Years

The best years that the URI Rugby Club ever had were from 1978 through 1979. There was a core of experienced ruggers playing during this time that had played together for a few seasons. The pack was strong, had good size and height, and covered the pitch well. The backs that were always fast with each new configuration over the various seasons, seemed to be at their best during these two years, before Rob left us. Also, we played many men's rugby clubs, not just college teams.

In 1979, we won both the prestigious Harvard Business School and New York Sevens tournaments and we lost to the Denver Barbarians men's club in a national sevens championship match final held in Connecticut. We made it to the semifinals of the New England Rugby Union open fifteens tournament that same year losing to the eventual winner – the Boston RFC men's club which was dominant against men's teams when I played.

The article below was in "The Providence Journal" newspaper after we made the semifinals in that New England Tournament at the end of the spring season.

URI rugby team makes semifinals

PROVIDENCE — The University of Rhode Island's rugby team posted a pair of victories yesterday and advanced to today's semifinal round of the New England Rugby Football Union Tournament at Hope High School.

URI defeated Berlin, Conn., 12-4, in its opening round, then shut out the Harvard Business School, 15-0, in a quarterfinal match. The Rams will play the Boston Rugby Club, the defending tournament champion, in the semifinals this morning at 11 o'clock.

The Providence Rugby Club, the host team of the tournament, was beaten by Boston in the quarterfinals, 13-3. Warren Boothman scored Providence's only points on a penalty kick. In its opener, Scott Swanesey intercepted a pass and ran 50 yards for a try, giving Providence an 8-4 victory in double overtime over Portland, Maine. Tom Nasca also scored a try for Providence.

Brown University lost to Beacon Hill, 8-7, in its opening round match. Beacon Hill will play Hartford in the other semifinal match. The championship game is scheduled for 3 p.m.

We did lose some matches especially when injuries occurred to important players or some teammates couldn't play on a specific Saturday because they were playing with the New England Select Side or they might have been trying out for this special all-star team on a URI match day. Every week, you had to bring your "A" game and the best players. Rugby was quite competitive then between both college and men's club teams. Below are some of the final scores of "blowout" matches only that occurred on or around these years. We did put up many points on offense and didn't give up many points on defense – a simple strategy to win in any sport.

Fifteen-a-side

Harvard University 22 to 4

Yale University 25 to 0

Brown University 34 to 9

Cortland State University 64 to 6

Coast Guard Academy 42 to 0

Boston University 45 to 0

Hunter College 32 to 0

University of Connecticut 42 to 6

Columbia Business School 56 to 0

University of Vermont 42 to 3

Wesleyan University 53 to 0

(Payback from the first rugby match I played in!)

Long Island men's club 32 to 3

Groton Rugby men's club 46 to 3

Charles River men's club 54 to 0

Springfield men's club 20 to 0

White Plains men's club 34 to 6

University of New Brunswick 37 to 0

("The Big Red Machine" from Canada)

Seven-a-side

Beacon Hill men's club 26 to 0

Charles River men's club 24 to 0

Connecticut Bushwackers men's club 30 to 6

Washington Exiles men's club 30 to 4

Central Connecticut State 42 to 6

(Finals of NY Sevens)

'78 SPRING SCHEDULE

R. I. RUGBY CLUB

DAY	DATE	OPPONENT	SITE	# SIDES
Sat	4-1	Univ. of Connecticut	Away	3
Sat	4-8	Mystic River	Away	3
Sat	4-15	Providence	Home	3
Wed	4-19	Harvard	Home	3
Sat.	4-22	Long Island	Home	3
Sun	4-23	Coast Guard Academy	Home	2
Wed	4-26	Boston College	Home	3
Sat	4-29	Charles River	Away	2
Sun	4-30	Western Mass Univ.	Home	2

BUSCH BEER

The 1978 spring schedule above was a wallet size version that one of our ruggers created for the team. Notice the beer advertisement – did the team pay for this promotion or did the Busch distributors pay us?

Rugby

None of the players are on scholarship. There is very little press coverage, besides the Cigar. But the URI Rugby Club had the most successful year of any URI sports team.

The spring season for the Rams was the best in the six year history that Rugby has been played at this school. The Ruggers finished the season with a 8-0 record, outscoring opponents by the unbelievable total of 287-26.

In addition to the on-field heroics, the Ruggers continued their now legendary tradition of the post-Rugby game parties where the home team provides a keg for the visiting team.

Highlights of the season include a hard-fought 30-10 victory of the Providence Rugby Club, a 17-6 victory over a tough Yale squad, a 21-0 victory over arch-rival Brown Rugby Club and in the season finale a surprisingly easy 37-0 shut-out over the University of New Brunswick Rugby Club. (C.H.)

J. Greenwald

The "79" URI yearbook article above showered the Rhode Island Rugby Club with plenty of praise and compared us to all the other "official" sports teams (not just club teams) during that specific year.

URI rugby club hits the big-time

By TIM COTTER
Times Sports Writer

A couple of weeks ago the Vermont Rugby Club traveled six hours to Kingston to play the Rhode Island Rugby Club. After the game, some of the Vermont players were asked why they would travel so far to play rugby. "We want to be in the big-time," one player responded.

The player wasn't joking either, because as far as college rugby goes in New England, URI has reached the big-time.

The past two seasons URI has finished third in the New England tournament behind the Boston and Beacon Hill Rugby Clubs.

Boston and Beacon Hill are "city" clubs while URI is a "college" club. City clubs are comprised of older players, veterans of the game. College clubs are comprised mainly of college students, newcomers at the game.

The Rhode Island Rugby Club, its official name, is a college club comprised mainly of URI students.

No college club has ever won the New England title and URI's third-place finish is the best ever by any college club in recent years.

But despite URI's success city teams are reluctant to play them. Most city clubs see it as a no-win situation when they play college teams.

Rhode Island instead has had to be satisfied with playing other college clubs. While doing so it has dominated the New England rugby scene, rolling up a two-year record of 24-1. Its only loss came this year to Harvard Business School.

This article was in the Narragansett Times, a local town newspaper sometime in the spring of 1979. Even though we played both men's and college clubs, we had quite a record against the college teams at the time. Our dominance actually hurt us from scheduling some of the men's teams – they didn't want to lose to a college team. Our record was 24 and 1.

Sid

The University of Rhode Island's mascot is the ram but the URI Rugby Club's mascot when I played was a very large, good-natured, German Shepherd, mongrel dog named "Sid". Sid's owner was Joe Rock but much of the time Sid traveled by himself and followed the ruggers and other students all over campus. He was well behaved at home matches and I don't think Joe used a leash for Sid. Sid sat or lay on the ground and watched many of the rugby battles. Sid also attended the post parties if dogs were allowed in the buildings. He was one of the guys although we did have to limit his beer intake.

Joe and a friend with Sid smiling for the camera in the photo above.
(Photo by G. Desisto)

The Last Season

I moved back home and was living with my parents in the fall of 1980 while returning to school for a few computer technology classes at the local community college in Warwick, Rhode Island. Looking forward to a new career, I also caddied at a nearby golf course for some needed cash. My Ford Pinto had broken down and I used my parents' car when it was available and I needed to travel. I rode a new ten speed bike, a present from Jeannie when working at the golf course. This is the same golf course where I met Governor Joseph Garrahy the following year who was then in his last term as governor of Rhode Island.

I was caddying for two businessmen and the Governor was in the same foursome. After the first few holes, the Governor started a conversation with me and asked me about my schooling and current profession. I told him about my work history and my current computer classes while I searched for a new job. He felt bad for me after asking me what I was up to and he told me to drop off my resume at his office; I had already filled out a job application with the state. A week or so later, I received a phone call from the Department of Administration and was scheduled for an interview for a technology position within this same office. I completed a short written test during the interview process and was next offered a job that I accepted right away and my new career began. **Thank you again Governor Garrahy!**

My final rugby season occurred with the Providence Rugby Football Club in the fall of 1980 because URI was much too far to travel and I was very busy with school at that time. They were a very good men's team and a great bunch of guys. It was strange playing with Bob and John Hoder, Rocco, Turkey, Panda, Gerry, Jeff, Kent, Mike, Dr. Tom, Cags, and the rest of that team that we used to compete against even though it was mostly against their "B" team in my early rugby career. I also missed the Rhode Island backs that I was so accustomed to playing with for so many seasons. My other sport, karate took over the rest of my free time, so I stopped playing rugby then and that very large part of my sports life was over.

This photo shows me in the Providence RFC uniform preparing to kick the ball away, hoping to retrieve the ball before the other full-back or wing could get to it. I remember the Hartford RFC match when this offensive play actually worked. The ball took a perfect bounce and I caught it in full stride and scored. It's funny how you remember the good plays and forget most of the bad plays. (Photo by a Providence RFC fan)

CHAPTER 13

The final chapter and rugby reflections

"It's not what you achieve, it's what you overcome. That's what defines your career."

Carlton Fisk – Retired Hall of Fame American baseball player and Boston Red Sox legend.

The article below was written by Bryan Ethier, a sports writer for *The Good 5 Cent Cigar* student newspaper in 1979. Many of our players were graduating and moving on and entering the real world. Some would continue playing for URI or other men's clubs where they relocated. Bryan enjoyed being a fan as well as an "objective" writer. He currently is an author of various non-fiction books and novels and now lives in Connecticut. Bryan gave us some great press and his descriptions of some of our matches and players were legendary.

Dave Lavallee was another "Cigar" sports student reporter who covered the Rhody Ruggers during my playing days. He is still enjoying his days with the University of Rhode Island where he is currently employed as an Associate Director of the Communications and Marketing Department.

The Good 5 Cent Cigar URI Rugby article, 1979 - Bryan Ethier

"Rugby is unequivocally a great sport. I think I called last spring's URI Rugby Club every adjective from superlative to super human. They didn't beat teams, they cruelly destroyed and terminated the life out of each and every opponent they played. There was a stretch in the season where they had outscored their opponents by something like 250–20 margin. They were indeed phenomenal.

There were many reasons for their success. Names like Calissi, Tagliardi, Reynolds, Chase, Murphy, et al., were gossiped by those following the rugby circuit. They were unbelievably fast and especially quick.

What was most amazing about the team was that they didn't relax on the field and loaf. They worked for their wins. At the end of each game, every player was brown and green, and looked like something the cat dragged in from the garden. And of course, there were the cuts and bruises, which were as frequent as their birth marks and freckles. And there was reason for that. They dove with their heads and arms at opponents' galloping legs and pumping thighs. They appeared to have no fear, at least they never showed any on the field. There were numerous times when the captain Mike Tagliardi had to be scooped off the field with a soup ladle borrowed from ROJO's. He'd get physically mangled, and bits and pieces of his body would scatter – nose on Beck field, chin on Meade field, and legs three feet under. But he'd get up and shake it off, somehow they were all like that.

There was the speed of the backs too. Connor Murphy, when flipped the ball via eight zillion players, would pick up speed and streak down the field literally. There'd be shorts and a shirt and a pair of semi-human looking socks back at the ten-yard line and a blur flying by sending partisan fans flying into the wind like crisp autumn leaves from the tornado-like gusts he created.

And of course, there was the scrum, the mid-afternoon get together of the bulls, bison, and saber toothed tigers. Bound arm in arm, cheek to cheek, they'd wrestle for the ball which would eventually squirt out of the pile, like a slippery, slimy pig from a mud bowl. All this would lead to a try, which is Swahili for touchdown.

Then of course, there was halftime and the tapping of the kegs and instant glee for the fans, of which there were always tons-worth. The kegs became a gathering for everyone. By the time the second half commenced, everyone was fruit looped…

The ruggers were indeed hard to stop."

The years have come and gone and our rugby days are over but some of us still gather as a team twice a year or so and rehash many of the matches and party festivities as if they occurred last week. Funny thing about rugby history, we get better as a team and individually as more years go by and we might even embellish a little on some of the stories that are told.

Some of us stopped playing rugby and our careers ended when we graduated from the University of Rhode Island but others played for a few more years on other men's rugby club teams. Even those players that later competed on other teams seem to enjoy the URI get-togethers better than the other rugby club functions or reunions. This was our first taste of rugby when we played at URI, the game that none of us expected to play but somehow discovered it and gave it our all.

"Give Blood, Play Rugby" and we did.

The photo above shows the team after one of our New England Tourney matches in 1980 (my last URI tournament). We were quite happy – it must have been after we won a few matches to reach the semifinals. Pictured from the top to bottom row are: Tom Lake, John Gianni, me, Reed, Mike D, Soup, Paul T, Dan, Will, Dave G, Ben Stevens, JTags, Kent, Lenny T, Ricky, Tats, Howie, and Wes.(Photo by G. Desisto)

"A trophy carries dust. Memories last forever."

Mary Lou Retton – Retired United States Olympic Gymnast and Gold Medal winner.

I emailed some of my rugby teammates who I stay in contact with over the years – during my work on this sports book project – and mentioned that I wrote a book about our team and that the book had received some positive feedback from two publishers who liked it.

At that time the manuscript didn't make the final selection cut but I kept on searching for the right publisher for our true story and months later, Austin Macauley took a chance on an unknown author and offered to publish this book. I share a "group" email list with many of these old ruggers and we chat from time to time between our reunions.

The "boys" thought it was an interesting idea to write a book about the "team" but also wondered who and what was in it. I sent them a few sample chapters and photos and some of them sent me back their short stories and memories in emails. Below are just a few of the other Rhody Rugger's best memories or feedback on the book excerpts. I did do some minor editing for grammar and content to make sure these bullet points match the theme and format of this story. We all had favorite memories during our playing days with the Rhode Island Rugby Club and some of theirs are below. The ruggers older than me seem to remember the early foundation years playing against other colleges, not so much the men's team matches or the special sevens tournaments.

Nags

Some notable times: the violent battle vs. Boston University at the Yankee Conference college tournament in Sept 1975 and the subsequent repeat match again vs. Boston University in March 1976. Rob remembers those tough games very well.

The UMass match in the spring of 76 when I came out of a ruck (when a ruck was a ruck) and a UMass player in his nice white uniform looked like he was shot and was bleeding from his rib cage – I still would like to know who bit him! If I remember correctly, you scored a long try up the sideline in that game.

The Winter Park men's club match in Florida in 1976 in 100 degree heat.

The Springfield men's club game on a Friday night that ended up in multiple fisticuffs, whereby Jake went out of the game with a completely swollen and shut eye.

The matches vs. Brown University were always difficult.

The Friday night game vs. Springfield where Cass lost his front teeth, Harry dislocated his shoulder, two other players were seriously hurt and we finished the game with 13, really 12 players. Harry stayed in the match but couldn't do anything and we still beat those guys with a score of 18 to 9.

Doug Fay scoring a 55 meter drop kick vs. BC (Boston College) where the ball sailed over my head and I thought no way will it make the goal post, but damn, it did – greatest kick I have ever seen.

One Saturday morning, spring of 77, Rob comes to my dorm room at Fairweather early and tells me we need to line the field for the afternoon game. So we go out to beyond the practice football fields, get the groundskeeper to give us lime, the spreader, measuring tape, and string. I ask Rob for the dimensions – 100 by 60? He says no – 110 by 70. Well, we do the length 110 yds. and then get to the width. Rob says let's do 75 instead, and when we get to 75, he says 80 yds. is better. I just start laughing. Needless to say we played Coast Guard and our backs that day had a field day with the space they craved.

I could go on and on but the most notable times were the rugby parties with Lenny "Cowboy" Dawson and Doug Fay leading us all in song.

Jake

A few added notes to the matches above. After the BU bloodbath rematch in the spring (where we had to put up the goal posts ourselves, way in the back of the main fields because it was too early for teams to be on the fields yet), BU lost several players for the season. When we saw them at the end of the season at the Harvard 7's, they mentioned they had some guys just coming back then – share and share alike.

Also, after losing sight in my eye at the Springfield Friday night game, I was coerced into refereeing the URI match the next day (vs. who I can't recall) with one eye only.

For another memorable game, who was it that we played at South

Kingstown High School (Was it St. John's?) in the snow? We plowed the sidelines and goal lines and let it go from there.

Reed

Yea Jake – it was St. Johns. It was fun for awhile but then somehow, I got recruited to play in the "C" game which I think was a sevens match due to a lack of numbers. The novelty of playing in the snow had worn off by then. I was still cold and wet from the earlier game.

I rode back to campus on the St. John's bus. It was a regular yellow school bus just like the one you may have rode on in elementary school except this one had a men's room on it which consisted of a plastic funnel taped to the rail by the front door with a length of plastic hose running down the stairs through the rubber seal in the door. Pretty clever, I thought. Beats passing around a plastic gallon jug riding in a van which I remember some doing on one of the real long road trips. Naturally, it got knocked over at one point.

Cowboy

There were some hijinks before you joined the club as well. The usual stuff at parties, Rugby Queens/Alouette, a URI Invitational Tournament in the fall of 1974 and a memorable road trip to Wesleyan University in the spring of 1975.

Plus, our glorious 3rd place finish in the Harvard Sevens Tournament at or around the same time. We lost to the Harvard Business School, the eventual winner. We arrived at the tournament with no subs and registered the URI club that same day.

Soup

It is amazing to me how you can still recall all of the details about the games. I didn't think the Cigar articles included that much detail. Did you keep a diary back then?

Rob

I am really enjoying all the comments.

Doug

I'm sure glad you all have great memories because I live vicariously through them. I think I lost part of my wits when I got kicked in the face in the Boston University bloodbath…

I don't remember Corie Joseph but I know I beat his high school football team 21-14 in the fall of '71! I remember that game well because I threw my best pass of my life to Peter Suorsa down the left side, probably 40 - 50 yards downfield and hit him in the hands and he dropped it.

Barry R

The picture at the end is great. You know it was Cole in that picture who first told me about Rugby. I was in the weight room working out one day after football season ended and I knew Cole and met him there, asked him what he was doing etc. He told me about rugby practice starting. The rest is history and I will never forget him. It was all great.

The story about the Harvard Sevens game against Holy Cross brought back the most memories. I remember that game like it was yesterday. We had such a great tournament that day. I can still remember that loss to Holy Cross. Very disappointing then and it still is, however so nice to bring it back.

I can't believe everything that you guys remember from those rugby days. It all brings back great memories. I just wish now that I had played with you guys in the fall season and I also would have enjoyed going to Florida with you.

Dirty Harry

Good morning Connor. Enjoyed reading your excerpts, had me laughing. So who was our athletic muffin man who hardly ever lost? Also, thanks for making me sound tougher than I was.

In regard to the Winter Park game, I think Bennett broke his arm as he came to the aid of one of our players approximately two or three minutes into the game. Also, I remember hearing that Winter Park was banned from tournaments due to constantly fighting so that didn't take long to happen in our game. I also remember Rob wearing more than just a pair of shorts to start the game and early into the second half asking me to remind him to remove the extra layer at half-time. I still remember my response, "Sure, but that was 10 minutes ago." Guess Rob had a concussion or was suffering from the heat.

But Rob was also his normal self and had a great play at the end of the game to save a win. He kicked the ball out of the hands of one of their players inside the goal area and out of the try zone. Winter Park couldn't believe what just happened.

Steak

Many thanks for sending the photos. The newer one is a bit scary. Who are those guys? I believe I have a copy of the one when we were younger, but not in digital format. The article was very interesting. Who knew?

Peter B

Congratulations! Awesome news. Like so many other comments, it is amazing what you can recall. I have trouble remembering what I did last weekend! I look forward to a book signing party!

Mike T

Regardless, if the book ever gets published, in reading it, it brought back some great memories. I think over the years, many of us have forgotten how really good we were. Each player brought their own unique set of skills to the field (and parties) and as a team, as the stats show, we were one tough team to beat and/or to score points on.

Sometimes, it feels like the days at URI were a long time ago and other times, it seems like yesterday - and I wouldn't trade the memories or friendships I made, for anything.

Mick

Thanks for the pics, I had a lot of hair...

I agree with Harry, put in the real stuff and you're on your way to Hollywood. It was good seeing you. Let me know when I can get a copy of the book.

Reed

Hey Connor, look what I found. I think it's the same mug from the Harvard Sevens photo but somewhere along the way the nameplate went missing. I mean it has been 37 plus years or so. The medal next to it is what the French team's executives presented to us before we played that all-star match.

EPILOGUE

I'm sixty-two years old now and don't play rugby anymore and to be honest, I can't remember my final match playing for the Rhode Island Rugby Football Club or the Providence RFC but I still miss this game. One of the URI ruggers recently sent me some information concerning an "Over 59" rugby tournament and other men's age group competitive rugby teams including an "Over 79" grouping. These ruggers must be very serious and quite healthy although the rules are modified of course depending upon the age group. This does not interest me at all. Rugby is largely a physical contact and non-stop running game especially with the backs and at my age and with my previous injuries over the years, I know my limitations.

I currently play basketball in an over forty town league with a great bunch of guys in the fall and winter run by Chris Anderson, a young forty-year-old who can still drain the deep three pointers. I compete in Masters Track in the triple jump and discus in the summer (Track is a very humbling sport.), primarily working on personal bests in each event. I still work out on my own doing many of my Tae Kwon Do katas or forms and spar with imaginary opponents but I stopped competing in karate tournaments many years ago. I also enjoy watching all my favorite sports teams on television – Celtics, Patriots, and Red Sox.

Very little with sports has changed for me since I was a small boy growing up in Riverside and joined my first little league baseball team when I was in grade school, played pick-up "street hockey" in high school on grass in my friend's backyard with tennis balls instead of plastic pucks, or played competitive soccer in an over "40" state league when I was much older. It will all end at some point (The mind is willing but the body sometimes isn't.) but for now, I'm still playing games, competing, and still having FUN! **Please, don't tell my mom.**

In this photo, I'm standing next to my brother Eddie preparing for the Memorial Day parade in our town. The local Little League baseball teams were a large part of this event. I was only five years old and Eddie was ten. I'm not sure where they found the uniform for me because in 1960, organized Little League didn't start until ages eight or nine. I was so proud to be a part of a team even then. Eddie played various sports growing up and I looked up to him and followed his lead. He excelled in track and was very good in high school and college. He also attended URI and after graduation, he became a high school history teacher and guidance counselor, as well as a track coach. He was inducted into the Rhode Island Track Coaches Hall of Fame a few years ago. (Photo by B. Murphy)

August 2013 – Harry's backyard, Jamestown Rhode Island.

From the top left to the bottom right of this photo: Harry, Chris, Jack, Danny, Ricky, Soup, Bags, Steve, Kevin, Frank, Bobby, and JTags – the real Rhody Ruggers. A few missing from the photo that day: Bobby R, Harry D, Steak, Gary F, Mike K, and Cowboy. (Photo by S. Seidler)

Below are some of the official Rhody Rugger signatures from the back of the inside cover page photo taken in 1976. If you attended URI during the seventies and followed any of the rugby matches, you might recognize the real Connor Murphy's name and some of the others.

APPENDIX A

Abbreviations and word key

URI – University of Rhode Island

BA – Bachelor of Arts, an undergraduate college degree

HBS – Harvard Business School

RFC – Rugby Football Club

USA Rugby - the national governing body for the sport of rugby in America and founded in 1975

Cigar – The Good Five Cent Cigar, the student newspaper of URI

Projo – The Providence Journal, the state newspaper of Rhode Island

"A's" – the number one team or varsity team of a rugby club

"B's" – the second team or junior varsity team of a rugby club

"C's" – the third team or second junior varsity team of a rugby club

IOC – International Olympic Committee

NFL – American Professional National Football League

USFL – United States Football League (now defunct)

NBA – American Professional National Basketball Association

NIT – National Invitational Tournament (college)

NCAA – National Collegiate Athletic Association

AAU – Amateur Athletic Union

Ivy League – the athletic conference comprised of sports teams from eight private institutions of higher education in the Northeastern United States

Title IX – legislation that requires schools that receive federal funds to provide girls/women with equal opportunity to compete in sports

ROTC – Reserve Officer's Training Corps

SEC – URI Student Entertainment Committee

Sensei – an instructor of the martial arts

Tae Kwon Do – a Korean martial art noted for its kicking techniques

Kenpo – a Chinese martial art noted for its many hand techniques

Dunes Club – a seasonal beach club for members only where many of the URI students worked during the summer

ROJO's – Roger Williams Dining Hall on the URI campus

Streaking – the act of running naked through a public place

Quad – URI's heart of the campus, a small grass field surrounded by trees with brick and cement walkways where students hang out and relax or walk across to get to various parts of the campus

Down the line – the location where many older URI students live; in the local towns and beach areas off campus

APPENDIX B

Rugby glossary

Listed below are a few of the basic rugby terms and definitions that should help anyone understand this unique game invented in England and that evolved into a distinct new sport in the United States in the early nineteen-hundreds – American football.

Match – A rugby game between two opponents.

Pitch – The field where rugby matches are played and it is usually 100 meters long and 70 meters wide.

Goal posts – These are the upright structures at the center of the try line. The cross bar is usually 3 meters from the ground, the side posts are usually 5.6 meters apart, and the height of the goal posts is a minimum of 3.4 meters.

Backs – This is the group of players who do not participate in scrums and lineouts, except for the scrum-half. These ruggers do most of the running in the match.

Forwards – This is the group of players that bind together into scrums, line up for lineouts, and are most active in the majority of the rucks and mauls (also called the pack).

Pack – This refers to the eight players that are called forwards and they are usually the physically larger players that comprise a scrum.

Scrum – This is an option in a match used to start play again after a minor infraction, usually a knock on or forward pass. The two opposing packs come together to create a scrum and the stronger or quicker side pushes over the ball to start the offense when the ball comes out "clean".

Binding – This occurs when rugby players lock hands and arms with each other during any scrum, ruck, or maul. This is necessary to combine strength with teammates and it also creates a larger obstacle for the opposing team to handle.

Sevens – This is the version of rugby where only seven ruggers play on the pitch at one time. It is usually seven-minute halves.

Fifteens – This is the version of rugby most commonly played with fifteen ruggers on a side and 40-minute halves. It is also called Rugby Union.

Back ten – When a penalty occurs, the offending team must retreat back ten meters from the mark on the pitch.

Conversion kick – This is the "extra" kick that counts as two points that occurs after a "try". The kick is centered where the rugger scores the try and ten meters from the goal line.

Forward pass – When a ball carrier passes the ball in front of himself/herself when trying to make an offensive move. This is also a minor penalty that results in a scrum down for the opposing team.

Knock on or knock-on – When a ball carrier drops or mishandles the ball forward out of his hands or arms from a pass or a kick. A penalty results in a scrum down similar to a forward pass.

IRB – This is the acronym for the International Rugby Board. This organization oversees and maintains and also updates if necessary, the Rugby Union laws and bylaws.

Lineout – This is the term used when the ball goes out of bounds in a match and the opposing team that was not responsible for the ball going out of bounds resumes the game with a "throw-in". Two rows of ruggers must line up perpendicular from the designated spot where the lineout is taking place and then they try to catch the ball when it is thrown back into play.

Throw-in – This occurs when the ball is thrown in during a lineout, signaling that play has resumed.

Mark – This is the spot that is determined by the referee where a scrum takes place.

Maul – This occurs when a ball carrier is tackled by the opposing team but remains standing upright and does not go to the ground.

Ruck – This occurs when a ball carrier is tackled by the opposing team and falls to the ground. The player then must release the ball and both teams try to gain possession of the ball.

Drop goal – This type of score occurs when a player drop kicks the ball through the uprights while play is still going on. The team is awarded three points for this type of goal and it is sometimes called a "field goal".

Place kick – After a penalty, kicking for goal can occur while the play is stopped. This type of score is also worth three points.

Try – This refers to the main method of scoring during a rugby match. This only occurs when the ball carrier grounds the ball into the opposing team's in-goal zone. It does not count as a try to just cross the goal line, the method in American football. This score is worth five points.

Tunnel – This is the invisible space between two opposing rugby teams during a scrum down or lineout.

In-goal area or goal area – This is the area that covers the ends of the pitch between the try line and dead ball line and it is where the ball must be touched down to score a try.

Dead ball – When a play stops for any reason during a match, the ball becomes a dead ball. If the referee determines a dead ball, then any action that happens after this is nullified.

Try line – This is the line that indicates the start of each team's in-goal zone.

Offside – This is a term for whenever a rugger makes a play on the ball from an illegal starting position. This can happen throughout the match because the ball continually acts as a moving line of scrimmage.

Referee – This is the only "acknowledged" official who oversees a rugby match. The referee is also the timekeeper.

Send-off – When a player engages in ongoing dangerous or harmful play, then the player is ejected from the match. This player becomes a "send-off" and cannot be replaced by another player. The team with the send-off then plays the rest of the match with one less player.

Sin bin – If a player repeatedly commits major infractions of rugby rules or a player commits one extreme penalty or infraction, that rugger is sent off the pitch and stands in the area behind that player's in-goal zone for a time determined by the referee. The team that owns this player also plays short one player until the player is allowed back into the match.

Stoppage time – Any time the play is stopped because of an injury, it is called stoppage time and this downtime is added on at the end of the half where it occurred. This type of time is similar to soccer extra time.

APPENDIX C

Rugby position definitions

The various rugby positions have changed names over the years and these positions are known by different names in different countries. Below is what the University of Rhode Island RFC called these rugby assignments when I played.

Scrum-half – the back player who connects the backs to the pack and starts an offensive play after a clean "out" from a scrum.

Fly-half – the back player who is usually the first to receive the ball from the scrum-half and is considered the "quarterback" of the team. (He/she also passes and kicks well.)

Inside center – the back player who stands next to the fly-half and is usually a strong, larger size player who can run inside plays.

Outside center – the back player who stands next to the inside center and is usually a fast runner that possesses good ball fakes and can run both inside and outside running plays.

Wing – the back player who is usually the fastest player on the team and is sometimes the last back to touch the ball in a formation. (He/she is considered the designated try scorer.)

Full-back – the back player considered to be the last line of defense and is also adept at kicking the ball.

Hooker – the forward player who controls the ball and "hooks" it back to his own teammates in a scrum to start an offensive move.

Prop – the forward player who holds or "props" up the hooker.

Lock – the forward player also called second row who "locks" into the props.

Flanker – the forward player also called wing forward who "binds" with the locks on the side of the scrum and binds the major part of the scrum. (He/she also breaks away from the scrum and runs with the ball.)

Number eight – the forward player who completes the scrum and helps create a better, stronger push. This player also can break away from the scrum quickly and easily and can run with the ball.

APPENDIX D

Common rugby penalties

Rugby penalties that occur during a match may include such actions on the pitch as:

- if a player does not retreat at least ten meters at a designated penalty location
- if a player is offside and does not attempt or show any effort to move to an onside position
- if a player fails to release the ball after being tackled, or the tackling player fails to release the opposing tackled player
- if a player blocks an opponent – similar to an American football block
- if a player enters a maul or a ruck from the side
- if a player deliberately collapses either a maul or a scrum
- if a player performs a violent or inappropriate play such as: punching, scratching, elbowing, kicking, head butting, tripping, biting, etc.
- if a player deliberately throws the ball forward or out of bounds
- if a player drops or knocks the ball forward
- if a player deliberately leaves one's feet in a ruck
- if a player holds or tackles an opponent who does not have possession of the ball
- if a player obstructs an opponent in some way from tackling the ball-carrier
- if a player vigorously contests or argues a referee's decision or uses abusive language or behavior towards an official during the match

APPENDIX E

URI Rugger hangouts

Campus social gatherings between classes and on weekends:

Hanging out at the Memorial Union and other areas. (All photos by Yearbook staff)

Food and games during the day.

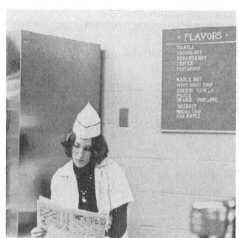 

Dancing on Friday nights in the Ram's Den and the "Pub", any night.

Studying hard at the campus library.

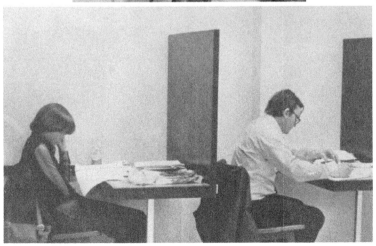

Concerts and other games.

Enjoying "Down the Line" activities year round:

Traveling to a few different locations off campus and renting a real house.

Visiting the surrounding taverns and clubs for more socializing.

And just relaxing.

APPENDIX F

Ruggers off the pitch

Mike V and Reed are in the photo below taken at a URI Rugby Halloween party. Mike was an Arab King and Reed was a hippie ghost with a beard. I am with my girlfriend in the right photo who later became my wife – it's obvious what we were at this same party. (All photos by friends)

My friend Steak visited me on a break from the Peace Corps in this photo. The background is the deck of the "Dunes Club" where I worked that summer.

The backs always hung out off the rugby field. In the photo below are a few at one of the early rugger weddings before the party started – so serious. Mike D, JTags, Soup, Rob, and Will. (Photos by L. O'Neil)

This photo shows the small band that played at another rugger wedding. But this is not just any band, the groom Wes is playing the tuba on the right. A few of the ruggers married right after graduation and were still playing rugby.

At the same wedding, Kathy C and Gail are probably not talking about any rugby matches. Kathy was Ricky's girlfriend at the time and a few years later they were married. (Photo by L. O'Neil)

In the top photo below, in front of the "Dunes Club" again, I'm in the middle of two of my fraternity buddies – John Staulo and Joe Torrealday. Both played for the URI Lax team and were working out on the beach that day. (Photo by a friend) The bottom photo shows a Sigma Nu fifties theme party before the women arrived with a "group selfie" taken the old fashioned way. The ruggers in this photo are: Vinnie – third from the left, and me – fifth from the left in the second row from the bottom. Steve Trailor had his eyes closed in the very top row – third from the right. (Photo by D. Avedisian)

In the left photo below, Tim is holding a Greek Week trophy; the right photo shows Ted and Ernie Ferrier at one of the Senior Week festivities in the rain. The bottom photo shows Donny Sifford with a friend and wearing his Rhody Rugby jacket at one of the URI football games. (Photos by Yearbook staff)

In the photo below, Paul T is exchanging pleasantries with some coeds at a yoga party.

This photo shows Ben Turner competing in the tug-of-war with his fraternity brothers during another Greek Week event. Notice his URI Rugby jersey. (Photos by Yearbook staff)

Tats on the far right, bottom row of this photo, was part of the SEC that brought concerts, movies, famous celebrities, etc. to the URI campus and provided entertainment for all. (Photo by Yearbook staff)

This final photo shows the back end of my Ford Pinto that I bought used when I started my teaching position at a private school in Providence, Rhode Island. Notice the bumper sticker on the left side of the trunk. An Irish national flag bumper sticker is on the right side of the trunk. (Photo by C. Murphy)

APPENDIX G

Rhody Ruggers over the years

Rugby attracted many different student athletes over the years when I played at URI. Some played for many seasons during their college days including myself but then others only played for a week or so because it just wasn't for them, including one of my cousins who tried it out for one day.

Listed below are some of the ruggers that I might have left out of this true story. Forgive me for forgetting or leaving out a few others – I played too many years at URI and with too many players. It is not intentional. It's been over 35 years since I have seen or heard from some of these Rhody Ruggers. Here's to all of them – past and present. They are all a piece of this rugby history.

Paul Dolan, Damon Navaro, Carl Bardy, Jerry Spina, Ralph Wordell, Al Maccarone, Glen Weaver, Jerald Schwab, "Red", Mike Bernnardo. Mike Gingerella, Cy Whitney, "A" team, Jay Sullivan, John Goding, Chris Conti, Bob Keneally, Jim Rose, Dave McCarthy, Steve Hall, Tommy Plummer, Brian VanCoughen, Dave Barrett, Howell Smith, Mattie Uustal, Peter Meade, "Chico", James Brunner, Paul Guerrette, Kevin Gajdeko, "Guts" Gunny, Ray Chism, Tom Ludic, Marc Nicol, Bill Grey, Paul Nonenmacher, Mike Tarasevich, Charles Adamopoulos, Tom Luitit, Frank Rack, Red Man, "E", Bob Campbell "2", Gary Faragelli, the Federico brothers, Brian Barnhart, New Wave Dave, Bob Gilmore, Tambo, Bob Coccia, the Cully brothers, etc.

GO RAMS!

APPENDIX H

A few sports updates

2016-2017 Olympic Rugby:

The USA men's rugby team didn't medal but Nate Ebner looked very good on the pitch. Fiji won the Gold medal by defeating Great Britain 43 to 7 and it was their first Olympic medal ever for this small island country – they looked great. The USA women's team didn't medal either. Australia won the Gold by defeating New Zealand 24 to 17 and the USA women placed fifth in the final standings.

Nate returned to the Patriots for the 2016 through 2017 NFL season and the New England Patriots won another Super Bowl with Tom Brady and company.

2016-2017 Rhody Rugby:

This past year was the 50th anniversary of college or men's team competition for the University of Rhode Island's men's Rugby Football Club. Coach Boothman (Turkey) and his assistant coaches began another season and hoped to return to the national spotlight for a shot at the National Division II College title by repeating as New England Conference Champions again. URI had a few tough loses and Norwich University went undefeated in the conference so they moved on to the Nationals. Keep the tradition going boys and let's try again next year!

2016-2017 URI Men's Track:

The URI men's Track and Field team won another Atlantic 10 Indoor Track Championship in the winter of 2016 that came down to the final event of the day. The team had then captured three consecutive conference indoor titles and five in the last six years for a total of 20 overall crowns in the school's history. They also won the New England 2016 Indoor Championship for a total of 20 New England titles in their division/conference. Congrats to Coach

Copeland and the team – one of the best kept secrets and success sports stories at the University of Rhode Island.

Below are two photos of the men and women's Track and Field A10 Conference Championship banners that hang in the Mackal Field House on the URI campus. (Photos by C. Murphy)

2016-2017 URI Men's Basketball:

The University of Rhode Island was ranked in both major national Division I preseason college basketball polls. The Rams were ranked No. 23 in the Associated Press and they were ranked No. 24 in the USA Today Coaches Poll. URI had not been ranked in any preseason poll for 18 years. Rhode Island plays in the tough Atlantic 10 Conference and they hoped to make the NCAA tournament for the upcoming season.

All the fans were ready for a great year and it happened. There were a few ups and downs along the way but in the end, URI won the A10 Championship and received an automatic bid to the NCAA Tournament. They won their first game by defeating Creighton University but then lost their next game to the Oregon Ducks with a close score of 75 to 72. Congrats to Coach Hurley and this tough and gritty basketball team!

Below is a photo of the official Basketball Hall Of Fame certificate for Frank Keaney who put URI Basketball on the map in the 1930s that resides in an older trophy case in Keaney Gymnasium. He was inducted in 1960.
(Photo by C. Murphy)

2016 - 2017 URI Wrestling:

The University of Rhode Island dropped this great sport and program in 1981 due to Title IX. This saddened many fans and friends of this Division I nationally ranked team. Wrestling came back as a club in 2013. Over the last fifteen years or so, other sports have been dropped at the university due to funding, etc. and became clubs. Many of these clubs compete with other colleges and can also vie for a regional or national championship.

John Staulo was voted into the National Wrestling Hall of Fame in Stillwater, Oklahoma this past December, 2017. This is a perfect tribute and award for a great high school and college wrestler as well as a great high school coach (Newton North High School, Mass.) who also mentors all his student athletes in and out of school!

'Stubby' is on the far right of the recent photo below from his inauguration banquet in April. It shows two other National Hall of Fame wrestlers and friends, from right to left: John, Dennis Fenton from UMass who also played football in the NFl for a few years after college, and Ray Miro (a Long Island native) – the previous great URI heavyweight prior to John and legendary Mount Greylock high school coach (Williamstown, Mass.) who was inducted a few years earlier. (Photo by C. Murphy)